D0908626

International Marketing Strategies

International Marketing Strategies

How to Build International Market Share

Erik Wiklund

McGraw-Hill Book Company

New York   St. Louis   San Francisco   Auckland   Bogotá
Hamburg   Johannesburg   London   Madrid   Mexico
Milan   Montreal   New Delhi   Panama
Paris   São Paulo   Singapore
Sydney   Tokyo   Toronto

Library of Congress Cataloging-in-Publication Data

Wiklund, Erik.
  International marketing strategies.

  Includes index.
  1. Export marketing. I. Title.
HF1009.5.W555 1987   658 8'48   86–21437
ISBN 0-07-070176-8

Copyright © 1987 by Erik Wiklund. All rights reserved. Printed in the United States of America. Except as permitted under the United States Copyright Act of 1976, no part of this publication may be reproduced or distributed in any form or by any means, or stored in a database or retrieval system, without the prior written permission of the publisher.

1234567890 DOC/DOC 8932109876

ISBN 0-07-070176-8

The editors for this book were William A. Sabin and Susan K. Tatiner, the designer was Naomi Auerbach, and the production supervisor was Thomas G. Kowalczyk. It was set in Baskerville by University Graphics, Inc.

Printed and bound by R. R. Donnelley & Sons, Inc.

For Kim, Erik, and John—with love

Contents

Preface

Breathtaking advances in information technology and communications, shrinking travel distances, sudden political and economic shifts, and the rise of new exporting nations are only a few of the forces that will shape international markets in the years ahead. You can expect an attractive but fast-moving and competitive marketplace that will test the effectiveness of veteran marketers and create challenges for eager newcomers.

How will you cope with the 1990s? What will it take to hold on to your best international markets and to capture new ones? Will you be sufficiently adaptive to sudden market pressures? Will you be ready to adopt computer-age game plans? I hope this book will help you find answers to these and other questions.

My earlier book, *International Marketing—Making Exports Pay Off,* was a guide for firms getting into the world marketplace for the first time—a step-by-step approach to setting up an export department. Modern technology notwithstanding, you cannot go international without knowing how to use basic tools, such as how to find and evaluate overseas agents. To build a kitchen table, you must know how to use hammers, saws, planes, and chisels. In international marketing the trouble is that too many companies are using basic tools unimaginatively. Too many people are trying to build the same kitchen table.

The basic tools of international marketing have not changed much over the years, and they are not likely to change significantly in the future. This book goes beyond basics. It assumes you already know how to use your hammers and chisels. Instead, it focuses on how to break away from the usual, routine patterns, particularly in critical areas such as market intelligence, the use of marketing personnel, in-house support, and strategic game plans. Its purpose is to help you refine your existing international operation and awaken you to the need to be creative in response to market opportunities.

If you are like most international marketers, you may be ignoring or misusing powerful weapons that are within easy reach. You may also be operating under policies and strategies that worked for you in the 1960s and 1970s but may now have become dangerously obsolete. Past successes can easily lull you into a false sense of security. In spite of modern communications, the speed of decision making in many firms today is not much faster than in the days of sailing ships. If in the last few years you have not constructively questioned and dissected every aspect of your international operations, you may run the risk of losing important markets to more creative and innovative competitors.

This book is mainly for executives and sales personnel in firms already involved in international marketing. It can also be useful to newcomers once they have learned basic principles. It will show how to spot and discard archaic policies and strategies and how to develop new approaches to markets and opportunities. You will learn how to gather and use real, live market intelligence, how to give added striking power to your sales force, how to squeeze added benefits from your in-house resources and talents, how to choose international targets wisely, how to avoid straitjacket policies, how to keep your international operation nimble.

In a quarter of a century of travel around the world, I have seen many eager newcomers gradually lose their momentum and become slow-moving bureaucracies. I have also seen large and small firms that always managed to maintain an air of innovation and creativity about their international operations, refusing to fall into monotonous routines. Both types of firms have made valuable contributions to this book.

I am grateful to my wife, Kathy, for her advice and her patience. Over the years she has joined me in dozens of meetings with business people throughout the world, invariably giving me the benefit of her unique talent for picking up on important details in people's behavior and attitudes which otherwise might have escaped me.

I also want to thank my son John for his enthusiastic help in performing many of the indispensable functions involved in putting a manuscript together, and for his welcome and gratifying moral support.

Erik Wiklund

1

"You'll Have to Find a Way"

Dianne Baker, field manager for Sirocco Windpower Generators, Inc., is flying home all psyched up over having finally hit upon a way to crack the Turkish market. In Istanbul she met Adnan Ozen, who seems to be the type of agent she has been looking for.

Together they have concocted a plan that may quickly put Sirocco in the picture. Municipal and provincial officials are gathering two weeks from now in the Black Sea city of Samsun to discuss low-cost energy sources—a unique chance for Sirocco to put on demonstrations for potential end users and decision makers.

Before leaving Istanbul, Dianne telexed her boss in San Francisco the outline of her plan. The following morning, in spite of a deadly eleven-hour jetlag, she shows up at the office bright and early.

"Look, Dianne," her boss says, "I've got a meeting to attend; let's talk after lunch."

"But we've got to move fast! You saw my telex?"

"Yes, yes. I glanced at it. A few hours can't possibly make much difference, can they?"

Dianne does her best to kill the morning by going through the paperwork that has piled up on her desk in the three weeks she has been away covering her Mediterranean territory.

At the meeting with her boss things begin to go sour. Ship three 1-kilowatt generators immediately? Contribute $2000 toward a show when there isn't even a promotion budget for Turkey? Send a technician at company expense to demonstrate the equipment? Appoint Adnan Ozen agent without any sales guarantees or at least a sales forecast?

Dianne fights for her plan for two days, but her initial enthusiasm quickly ebbs away. The home office is a tough nut to crack. Sometimes it seems so much easier to deal with a potential customer!

Eventually Dianne is forced to telex Adnan that there is no way they can participate in the show on such short notice, but she insists that Sirocco is

1

still interested in doing business with him. She is mailing him a letter with questions that have to be answered before he can be confirmed as Sirocco's agent in Turkey.

Six thousand miles away, in Sorocaba, Brazil, Paulo Correia gets a phone call from Sergio Andrade in Hong Kong. Paulo is export manager of Frangologia S.A., manufacturer of poultry-processing machinery. Sergio is a Brazilian free-lance market consultant covering China and Southeast Asia.

"I've just been to Hohhot in Inner Mongolia," Sergio says. "Their agriculture is booming, and I talked to people who are itching to start a modern chicken processing industry."

A one-week agricultural exhibition will begin in Hohhot in ten days, Sergio says. He wants Paulo to ship posters, films, slides, models of the various types of machines produced by Frangologia, and a technician who can assess project needs and suggest solutions.

"You don't give me much time," Paulo says.

"I know," Sergio replies. "Você vai ter que dar um jeito. You'll have to find a way."

Paulo does. But it takes him two wild days that extend well beyond regular office hours. He has to convince his managing director that the plan is worth the expense and effort even though it is at best a calculated risk. He has to personally scrounge around to gather all the promotional material and equipment. He has to talk the plant's chief engineer into diverting a top technician from a project in the State of Mato Grosso. He has to beg the head of the Varig Airlines cargo department for premium space on a flight that can make the right connections to Hohhot via Beijing.

But the job gets done, and the package is on its way seventy-two hours after Sergio's call.

If you have had anything to do with international marketing, how many times have you suffered Dianne Baker's plight? You fly home full of fire, only to learn that your enthusiasm is *not* contagious among the people in the home office. How many times have you and other overseas sales managers and salespeople been told that you must learn to see the forest instead of the trees?

How many times do you or your overseas sales managers allow Sirocco-type deals to fizzle out? Who is right—Sirocco or Frangologia? Is Sirocco committing a marketing blunder?

By all the rules of traditional international marketing, Sirocco is making the proper, accepted moves—acting prudently and refusing to respond emotionally to a plan which has not been carefully analyzed. Nobody in the home office can be faulted for sticking to established procedures and for playing it safe.

Frangologia S.A., on the other hand, is much more concerned with reacting quickly to any reasonable opportunity, even if it means rocking the boat, creating a few waves, and risking a minor financial loss.

Sirocco may have missed a chance to set foot in a new market. Frangologia may have scored a jump on its competitors.

What would *you* have done?

In international marketing there are times when it pays to be conventional and prudent. And there are times when it pays to be innovative, daring, and aggressive. Sirocco may have lost sight of the power of creative international marketing. Frangologia has not.

The very idea of creativity in international marketing flies in the face of carefully structured company policies. Creativity is *not* a gimmicky magic formula: It has to do with the ability to respond quickly and effectively to day-to-day, real conditions in the field.

Its ultimate goal is to improve your international marketing.

If yours is a seasoned international operation, you may feel quite smug with your worldwide performance. "Why," you may say, "last year our international business was up 13.5 percent! We must be doing something right!"

The real questions are: Did you use your resources to the hilt? Did your sales force pursue all the opportunities which came its way? Are you doing what it takes to get the most out of the markets you have penetrated?

Today's international marketplace is a small, tough, and competitive arena. More companies in more countries are breaking into world markets because the potential rewards are more enticing than ever. The competitive edge you need to win, or to do better, can come from perfecting a fresh, hard-hitting approach to markets and opportunities. If you don't find new ways to react to the pressures of today's markets, you may wake up one of these days with new competitors running circles around you.

The size of your international operation may be a reflection of past successes, but there is no guarantee that tomorrow you will be able to hold a lead over the competition. Success may have made you staid and stodgy. Having succumbed to bigness and the structuring that goes with it, you may have forgotten the importance of tailoring strategies to markets. You may have started as a hungry and pugnacious organization. Are you in danger of becoming a stagnant bureaucracy?

Smaller firms, including those which have barely made a dent in world markets, can be far more flexible and more personal in going after overseas opportunities their bigger and older competitors may have ignored. Firms which have gone international only in recent years, especially in Brazil, Taiwan, South Korea, Singapore, and India, are more likely than old-timers to understand the need for innovation and flexibility in marketing. They are not bound by traditions and archaic procedures.

The need for new, creative thinking in marketing is not only for manufacturers and suppliers. If you are an importer, a local wholesaler, distributor, or dealer, you can also gain from it. You are smack in the middle of the sales arena, but you may not always know enough about what is going w to cope with market developments. There is more. Are you ⎯⎯ped to seek out and evaluate manufacturers and suppliers whose products you would like to sell? Are you aware of the human and intelligence resources they may require before they can deal with you? What do you know about their marketing policies, personnel, reliability, competitiveness?

How to Lose Sight of
Trees *and* Forest

Excessive emphasis on "putting things in perspective" can quickly make you lose sight of real conditions in the international marketplace. Here are some dangerous symptoms to watch out for:

1. *Rigid company policies prevent effective tactics.* A good example has to do with assigning human resources to cover overseas market opportunities under a world pattern which simply ignores local conditions. The overall strategy is usually based on establishing geographic territories made up of regions or countries, not on a realistic assessment of opportunities. Personnel are wasted in the wrong places or not applied in sufficient strength where prospects are best.

Consider Smith & Welby, Ltd., manufacturers of hydraulic valves. Their master plan calls for systematically assigning field managers to key areas: Europe, Latin America, Africa, the Middle East, and Asia. Never mind the fact that most Latin American and African markets are down, and that all reports point to better conditions in the Middle East and Asia. Five people are hired and sent off to their territories, five shiny red pins are stuck in the world map in the international marketing manager's office in Manchester. The master plan is launched!

The result of this arbitrary assignment of human resources is that some of the field managers will find it difficult to cope with all the work which has to be done, while others will not have enough to keep them fully occupied.

There are many other examples of rigid central policies which ignore market conditions. Look at your own operation. Examine your marketing policies with a critical eye and ask yourself why they were created, what they have accomplished, and whether you really need them.

2. *Corporate international operations resulting from mergers and acquisitions increase the distance between a sales force and the individual companies producing the products.* This makes it hard to develop an environment suitable for innovation. The salespeople at one end, and the management of the producing companies at the other, seldom have any direct

contact with each other. Everything has to go through a corporate international office. Here is a typical case:

Mueller-Labo Gmbh is a conglomerate selling scientific instruments for educational, medical, research, and industrial laboratories. Originally each division was an independently owned company with its own export department. Today, exports are consolidated in a central office in Karlsruhe; the divisions have been completely shut out of all international business.

Field personnel report directly to Karlsruhe. Quotations for overseas customers are prepared by each division and submitted to Karlsruhe, where they are rewritten and passed on to overseas end users.

In addition to the confusion and delays brought about by having to channel everything through what amounts to a go-between office, there is another problem: Mueller-Labo's international field managers and salespeople are survivors of the personnel shakedown which followed the mergers. They don't all have the same background. Each sells the product line he or she sold before the mergers. For instance, Pieter Lange sticks to hospital equipment, Alan Wong to research and industry products. From the viewpoint of manpower utilization this makes sense. But while Pieter Lange concentrates on hospital equipment, nobody in his territory is promoting the other lines.

The consequences are obvious: Mueller-Labo is not doing as well as it should. There is room for improvement. Sales are being lost to inefficiency and because some products are being ignored in each market.

3. *International decisions are often made by poorly informed people far from the field, their thinking based on stale and skimpy market intelligence.* World markets are constantly changing. Look at the Third World. Most of it is sharply different from what it was fifteen years ago. The only thing we can say with absolute certainty about world markets is that they never stay the same. How does management keep up with developments? Where does it get the information needed to make serious decisions?

What kind of market intelligence are you getting? What do your executives really know about what is happening in the field? How much information reaches them? If your international organization is a pyramid of local and regional offices, each with its own set of executives, you run the danger of filtering out most of the nitty-gritty intelligence from the front lines before it has a chance to reach the main office. You may also be relying on intelligence sources which are totally useless—or unwilling to enlighten you!

4. *Too many decision makers at the top dilute effective marketing efforts.* The urge to refer everything to staff meetings or committees, to hide behind the anonymity of collective action, is a sure way to kill effective tactical marketing. Discussions on virtually any topic can take forever. Or they may generate masses of internal memos and reports. In this sort of

environment important issues, which should be quickly resolved, become bogged down in a morass of paperwork. A friend in Argentina calls this state of affairs a "burrocracia"—an organization so burdened with red tape and paperwork that in spite of modern technology it is unable to move faster than a burro.

Are you on the verge of becoming a burrocracia?

5. *Excessive structuring of an international operation leads to exaggerated emphasis on plans and manuals.* Here is a typical case of a company that paid more attention to "getting organized" than to the business of selling:

National Systematics, Inc. (NSI), decided to go international by acquiring a small firm of overseas manufacturers' representatives. Allan Johnston, marketing vice president at NSI, was put in charge of the company's brand-new international division. Meticulous to the extreme, he was shocked to learn that the reps he had just acquired had been operating without a sales manual!

He proceeded at once to remedy the situation, spending the better part of three months laboriously setting down precise rules and instructions on how to cope with every conceivable sales situation. The fact that he had never been overseas did not deter him. To run a proper sales department you needed a manual and that was that!

Eventually each rep received a binder with 200 pages of instructions, and a carton full of forms. There were forms to be used when composing a telex, expense account forms, weekly sales reports forms, monthly summary forms, pending quotations forms, travel expense forms, order forms, monthly and yearly forecast forms, budget forms, and forms to order more forms.

The reps screamed bloody murder. For several weeks chaos ruled, tempers flared, and sales came to a halt. Everybody was getting nasty telexes from Allan for using the wrong forms or ignoring instructions. Requests for legitimate information were often answered with a curt "Kindly refer to section IIIA/1 of your sales manual."

Finally Belkacem Zaouche, the Middle East rep, decided he'd had enough. He mailed in an order written on hotel stationery—a cardinal sin which prompted the following exchange of telexes several days later:

"Order improperly filed, suggest you study manual."

"Have donated manual to local sanitation department."

"Sending new copy by courier."

"Thank you but sanitation department requires no further copies."

Allan got the message. The manuals were never seen again. Belkacem went on to become the company's top field manager and a champion at creative marketing.

Beware of manuals! If you have one, is it helping your field salespeople, or is it stifling them? Is it a useful selling tool or just another attempt to exert control through petty administrative procedures? Ask your salespeople.

6. *Modern communications makes it easy to pass the buck.* When sailing ships took six months to get from Boston to Sydney, traders in distant outposts were on their own. Today, if you are an international salesperson, you can duck decisions with a short visit to the hotel's telex office. Let the home office deal with it, while you relax over a predinner drink by the pool. Home offices *always* have answers!

Passing the buck comes in handy when you, the salesperson, know full well that the answer is going to be "no." You can face a disappointed customer much more easily when a distant third party is responsible for the bad news. Who wants to be the heavy?

Of course, this timid approach dilutes field responsibility and initiative. An international headquarters that delights in making all the decisions and downplays local initiative will rapidly sap the strength of its sales forces and thus strengthen the competition's.

7. *Horse-and-buggy communications can be a destructive inside enemy.* It takes minutes to transmit 1000 words by telex or fax, seconds by computer. But there are two ways modern communications can be grossly wasted or misused. One is when a message is received and then meanders through a maze of internal procedures which have not changed much since the middle of the nineteenth century; the person to whom the message is intended may have to wait hours, if not a day or two, for the message to come up from the telex room. Another is when the home office uses modern communications to try to control everything that goes on in the field.

Modern communications and computer technology are vital ingredients in today's international marketing. Both are within easy reach of any company or individual. Make them work *for* you, not *against* you.

8. *The fear of taking risks promotes a don't-rock-the-boat frame of mind which does nothing to encourage initiative.* Who wants to make mistakes? Who wants them aired in public, even if the intention is constructive criticism? Not everybody has the guts of a Paulo Correia or a Belkacem Zaouche to stick his or her neck out and take a chance. Not every international marketing executive has the guts to let salespeople do their own thing and stand by them through thick or thin.

Do *any* of these eight symptoms apply to your company? To your home office, regional offices, and local branches? To your agents around the world?

Reaching for the Tactical Edge

Ignore the need for flexibility in international marketing and you will dilute your sales power, overlook opportunities, weaken distributor confidence and lose sales.

Your international operation probably started and continues to operate more or less like everybody else's. Certain basic rules have evolved over the centuries. You create an international or export division, hire field managers, set aside promotional budgets, identify priority markets, establish agents, perhaps set up branch or field offices, participate in trade shows, and do a number of other things by the book. Even pricing and discount structures within your industry are figured out more or less the same way.

This is all necessary and even vital. You can't go international and expect to do a job without the basic tools. So where do you go from there? How do you acquire the tactical edge? How do you push ahead of your competitors? The secret is to avoid or break away from the inertia of straightjacket policies and put more emphasis on what's happening in the field—the action zone. Use your basic tools creatively, imaginatively, and aggressively.

Laying down basic rules for creative international marketing is a contradiction, because it can easily lead to another confining straightjacket. However, there are basic techniques and practical steps to help you—manufacturer, exporter, distributor, importer, licensee, or overseas subsidiary—to gain the competitive edge. You can start adopting them today.

The four weapons of creative international marketing are market intelligence, human resources, productive logistics, and flexible game plans.

1. *Market intelligence.* A sharp in-house intelligence service can multiply the power of your field sales force. You are probably not getting more than a fraction of the intelligence you really need in order to make smart strategic decisions and launch hard-hitting tactical attacks.

2. *Human resources.* Look for untapped, undiscovered in-house human resources which can help boost your international sales. Learn to use your personnel where they will do you the most good.

3. *Productive logistics.* Creative international marketing can give your firm a striking power far beyond the size of your basic resources, if you know how to trim the fat from your in-house support staff and make everybody an active participant.

4. *Flexible game plans.* A few basic principles can help you develop the loose and flexible policies which allow tactics their full play. No management upheavals are necessary, even if your company has grown complacent about international marketing. You don't have to cast off centralized control. All you need to do is redirect and refine it.

In this book we will look in detail at these four weapons and how you can apply them practically and profitably, whether yours is a large or small firm.

International marketing involves a cast of characters whose roles and titles are not always clear or standardized. So let us get our signals straight on terminology from the start.

When I refer in this book to *marketing, marketing managers, field managers, salespeople, and sales forces,* I mean international. In the few instances when I mean *domestic,* I will say so.

The title *international marketing manager* covers a wide range of roles: export manager, vice president in charge of international operations, export sales manager, any number of other formulas, all intended to designate the person in charge of overseas sales.

The *field manager* is a fully employed person responsible for sales in an area consisting of one or more countries. He or she may be head of an overseas subsidiary, a branch or regional office, a network of local agents, company salespeople, or a combination of any of these. The field manager may reside abroad or back home.

A *salesperson* is someone fully employed by a manufacturer or exporter to promote and sell to overseas agents or end users. The salesperson may report to a field manager (the usual case in large companies) or directly to the home office (in a smaller operation). Field managers and salespeople are in effect a company's field sales force. Both functions involve considerable international travel.

An *agent* is an independent person or company selling your product in a country. The agent can be any of the many types of sales organizations needed to move products: an importer, wholesaler, retailer, commissioned representative, jobber, distributor, or dealer.

Networks of well-trained, well-informed, loyal agents are indispensable to international marketing, except where you have established your own full-time branches and subsidiaries. The principles and techniques which I discuss in this book apply to agents as well as to manufacturers and suppliers.

Let's begin with a fresh approach to market intelligence: what it is, why you need it, how you gather it, how you use it, and how you run it.

PART 1

Know Your Targets

2

An Ear to the Ground

You cannot sharpen your international operation without practical and thorough knowledge of markets, competitors, economic and business trends, agents, salespeople, field managers, export managers, end users, and decision makers. This is market intelligence—*the most neglected weapon of international marketing*.

Feed accurate and useful intelligence to your sales force and they will have a clearer picture of which targets to hit, when, where, and with how much power.

Companies are quick to appoint international marketing managers and salespeople. You may have ten or twelve field managers and presidents of subsidiaries scattered around the world. But do you have an international intelligence manager? Who in your company is in charge of shadowing the competition? The number of corporations with full-fledged intelligence divisions is still minuscule.

You need intelligence to help you figure out where and why your sales forces are going soft and losing ground to more aggressive competitors.

You need intelligence to find new markets, to hold on to the ones already cracked, to fight the competition, and to react quickly to sales opportunities.

You need intelligence so that you can make the best use of your marketing resources.

The need for intelligence is critical. The international marketplace is growing. There is more ground to cover every year, new nations eager to develop their economies, sudden shifts in political and economic conditions, awakened competitors no longer happy with domestic markets alone, and hungry newcomers from countries which have only recently become industrialized and export-oriented.

You may manage to do well with haphazard, unsystematic market information. You may think that you already know enough. Don't! Putting your trust in hunches and flying by the seat of your pants is risky. Insufficient intelligence can cost you sales. Poor intelligence is particularly deadly if one of your priority markets is a major, highly developed country such as the United States, Canada, Japan, West Germany, the United Kingdom, France, Italy, or one of the Scandinavian countries.

No matter how big your company may be, *you never know enough.*

Market intelligence is all around you if you know where to look and take the trouble to go after it. Gathering, evaluating, and using it does not call for any exotic skills; the job can be done by your present staff.

If you are an agent, you have an equally critical need for intelligence. You need it for two important reasons: to improve your own operations, and to strengthen your ties with the manufacturers and suppliers with whom you deal. Put yourself in the shoes of manufacturers and suppliers looking at your country and territory. Learn their intelligence problems and requirements. Try to understand and anticipate them. You will gain an edge over local competitors who cannot see anything except from their own narrow viewpoint. You will stand to gain in sales, profits, and prestige.

If you are an agent in a sophisticated major market you may have done nothing about serious intelligence, leaving it up to the supplier. This is a mistake because it weakens you and will eventually leave you in the position of not knowing as much about your own market as the suppliers you are dealing with.

Types of Intelligence

Some intelligence comes from your current research. It seldom includes useful, nitty-gritty intelligence straight from the field. If you are lacking this type of vital information, start by looking for it in your priority markets. It deals with what is happening *day by day* and comes from keeping an ear to the ground, not from poring over statistical tables.

These are the main uses of international market intelligence:

1. *To identify target countries.*   Even a far-flung international operation with ample resources must assign priorities and know where to apply maximum sales power.

2. *To stay alert to political and economic trends in the priority markets where you are already established.*   This can be critical, both to recognize new opportunities and to spot danger signals. For instance, not everybody was able to readjust in time to the changing conditions in Iran when the Khomeini regime took over. How did you make out?

3. *To decide what field and logistic resources you will need to break into new markets or expand existing ones.*   Only through careful intelligence evaluation can you estimate whether a market will require one, three, or five salespeople, a branch office, or agents.

4. *To plan international promotion geared to sales objectives and budgets.*   How much, where, and when to advertise; whether or not to go in for local trade fairs and conventions—another job which cannot be done

sensibly without factual intelligence. Learn all about local promotion schemes, even when you leave promotion up to an agent. This helps you develop better tactics.

5. *To budget the funds needed to accomplish reasonable marketing objectives*—a balance between what you want to achieve and how much you can afford to spend.

6. *To learn about the competition.* This is the main concern of intelligence. Learn all you can about the competition's policies, executives, sales forces, methods. Estimate how well your competitors are doing in local markets. Learn what prices and discounts will best respond to market conditions. How thorough and systematic is your current intelligence on your competition?

7. *To evaluate marketing outlets.* This is vital before you can appoint agents or decide to open up your own offices. It includes keeping track of and romancing the competition's agents. How many have you managed to entice over to your side lately?

8. *To evaluate end users or consumer groups and decide how best to get to them.* They are your ultimate targets. How you get to them is different in each country. Learn, through intelligence, how best to do it.

Are You Getting First-Class Intelligence?

What passes for market intelligence usually consists of tedious industrial and trade statistics. Computers are spewing out miles-long printouts that make some executives feel important but that are probably seldom read and digested. The more complex a market, the bigger the flow of trade statistics.

Many international marketing executives don't know what *real* market intelligence is all about. Here are some reasons:

1. *Ignoring the facts.* Once upon a time, the bearers of bad news were killed. Today what gets killed is bad news that doesn't agree with the views of top management.

A Texas manufacturer of scientific instruments made a sale to a Japanese research lab through a trading company. The equipment kept breaking down. The lab insisted that the problem was caused by local humidity. The manufacturer said "impossible, this never happens in Texas, where we have dozens of happy customers!"

The lab went on griping until the Japanese trading company, to save face, asked a local manufacturer to solve the problem. The instrument was modified, the research lab was satisfied, the Japanese manufacturer put the new and better version into production. Eventually it captured a good share of the Japanese market, leaving the Texas manufacturer out in the cold.

2. *An obsession with statistics.*   To most marketing executives, intelligence means government trade figures—good for long-range research but not too helpful in daily skirmishes with the competition. Official statistics are months old when you get them and may even have been made obsolete by political and economic shifts since they were gathered. Information retrieved from computerized databanks is not necessarily any more current. Much of it is taken from periodicals which themselves may contain months-old facts and figures.

U.S. embassy commercial officers in Nigeria, for instance, get official trade figures from the Nigerian government. The Nigerian government, like any other government, needs months to produce an updated report once or twice a year. The information which finally reaches the U.S. embassy in Lagos may reflect a situation which existed more than six months earlier. Several more weeks go by before the information is passed on by the embassy to the Department of Commerce in Washington, and made available to the public.

Eventually you will be able to get this type of data through a desk computer and a modem. But even then it will take humans to sort out and enter the data. If past performance is a guide, don't count on dramatic changes in the speed of human thinking in the next decade! In fact, it may slow down even further, as people become more dependent on computers and other modern technology.

3. *Missing and forgotten files.*   Most of the paper that goes into a filing cabinet seldom sees the fluorescent light of the office again. There is just too much of it in circulation in most offices, and one way to get rid of it is to file it out of sight. The more you file, however, the easier it is to forget what is in the files. Over the years I have produced reports on many overseas markets. I am no longer shocked when I run into a situation like this one:

"We'd like a report on the Brazilian market."

"I did one for you a few months ago."

"You did?" Pause. "Ah, yes, yes, I remember seeing it, now that you mention it. It must be here somewhere. I'm not sure we really had a chance to go into it. It was our busy season, you know! Could you send us a copy, anyhow?"

The computer is no help. Data filed on a diskette can be just as dead as in a file drawer. Since most computer files have to be coded, you can easily forget what a file contains unless you retrieve it regularly.

4. *Progressive dilution.*   This happens when information from the field goes through too many hands. What may start as factual intelligence ends up as a wishy-washy memo reflecting the opinions of all the people who had a nibble at it.

This may have happened to Wunderbra, a European brassiere manufacturer who launched a million-dollar TV campaign to conquer an Asian market. A consultant in the target country warned that the approach was wrong. Local women were not built the same way as the women in the manufacturer's home market, and they dressed differently. The main features of the European bra would be of no interest to them.

The consultant's warning was ridiculed. Wunderbra's smart advertising staff back at the home office knew better. The campaign was a flop.

What happened? Obviously nobody listened to the consultant. Perhaps the warning was watered down by home office executives who did not want their pet project knocked down or their views contradicted, so that when the message reached the decision makers, it was cast aside as an unimportant opinion.

5. *Too much emphasis on countries, companies, and products, not enough on people.*   Behind every company, every end-user organization, are flesh-and-blood people. Strangely, most companies seldom focus on the individuals involved in international marketing.

Your Latin American field manager telexes you:

"Nippon Latina, Ltd., extremely active, have taken our best dealers in Colombia and Venezuela."

Your first concern is to ask about prices, discounts, product features. But what about the people behind the Nippon Latina move? Is this part of an international strategy, or strictly field? Who is the Nippon Latina export manager? The field manager for Latin America? How is the company organized in the area?

These questions deal with people. You may have a lot of information about Colombia and Venezuela, and about the Nippon Latina products. Do you know anything about the people involved?

What's Wrong with Conventional Intelligence Sources?

One problem with market intelligence is that it usually comes from researchers who rely on a handful of publications and reports and seldom take the trouble to seek original, unusual, more creative sources. Another problem is that field intelligence is expected from unqualified, undependable, or erratic people. I am not trying to put anybody down. The sources you normally associate with intelligence gathering have other jobs to do, and no time or training to seek information. For instance:

1. *Government officials.* Either "country desk" officers in international trade departments, or commercial officers in overseas embassies.

They go for the general rather than the specific, they have to serve everybody, and they are not in a hurry. Tactical intelligence, however, has to be used quickly, with some urgency. It can't survive the slow pace of a multilayered government route from source to user.

2. *Agents.* Their job is to sell, not to do market research or gather intelligence for manufacturers. To rely on agents for intelligence is risky. They won't send you reports that make them look bad, or reveal important information about end users. A smart agent knows that marriages to manufacturers and suppliers are not forever.

Another problem with agents is that they don't always know enough about what is going on, and may rely on manufacturers and suppliers to put them in the picture. I cannot count the number of times in the last twenty-five years when I helped agents in Africa, Latin America, and Southeast Asia to find and contact the persons in charge of World Bank development projects in their own countries.

If you are an agent, you will have to decide how much information to pass on to the suppliers you deal with, how much to keep under your hat. This delicate balance requires a case-by-case assessment in which you should always put your own interests first. The more information you give suppliers, the better they will understand your market. This can result in stronger support to your own sales. It can also make the suppliers less and less dependent on you—a dangerous situation for you.

3. *Field managers and salespeople.* Collecting intelligence is only part of their job. Their mission is to sell. Field managers and salespeople don't always pass on information to the home office, for many reasons. They are not sure if management is interested. The information could make them look bad. Upsetting news may not be welcome back home. The information will clash with the opinions of a higher-up. They are sloppy about taking notes and keeping records. They have big territories, seldom spend more than three days in each country, and really don't have time to dig for grass-roots intelligence.

If management is erratic, and personnel are subject to being shifted, transferred, or fired unexpectedly, salespeople may be skeptical about telling too much to the home office. They may prefer to deal with management on a need-to-know basis, and keep most of the information to themselves.

4. *Traveling executives who like to be treated like royalty.* They seldom learn anything practical. They are entertained by field managers and agents. Their visits are announced well in advance. They see what their hosts want them to see. Good public relations, perhaps, but the views brought back can hardly be treated as factual intelligence.

5. *Executive and sales personnel who visit trade fairs.* They waste too much time looking at products and picking up catalogs, and don't spend enough time meeting people, finding out who's who in the competition.

What You Need to Know

Your intelligence service must define precisely what information will be useful to your sales force in the field and to executives who make decisions at the top. This goes for international marketing organizations as well as for local agents covering a country or a province.

In the search for new markets you need long-range information—reports and statistics from national and local governments, directories, institutions, libraries, foundations, and associations. It pays to keep searching for markets and to be ready to expand. This intelligence is a bore to gather and collate. Nobody likes to read it. But the job has to be done. You should already be getting this type of intelligence regularly.

Table 1 is a checklist of the information a company needs to identify new markets and keep up with international trends.

Your priority markets will demand a concentrated effort. If you focus on too many countries, even if your firm has the resources to sustain the operation, you will end up smothered by mountains of undigestible data.

If you are an agent and your territory is an entire country, you will face the same problem. Be realistic and assign priority to cities or regions where opportunities seem best. This selective approach applies in particular to huge markets like the United States and West Germany.

Aim your intelligence efforts at markets you have decided to penetrate right away, and those where you are already strong. *And at your competition.* Don't underestimate the need for nitty-gritty intelligence, even after you have established overseas offices or appointed agents, and the orders have started to come in.

Nowhere is intelligence more vital and useful than in markets you have already cracked. Nowhere do you need reliable sources more, to support, stimulate, and sustain aggressive sales forces. Table 2 is a minimum checklist of the intelligence you need to do the job.

Use the tactical checklist as a starting point; be flexible and imaginative. You need to know more than the names and addresses of agents. Find ways

Table 1. Strategic Intelligence Checklist

A. General

Industry worldwide exports

Main producing/exporting countries: shares of world market; export trends in recent years; leading markets (countries of destination)

Exports from "new" producing countries

Countries receiving development loans

Location and dates of leading international trade fairs

Main importing countries: import trend in recent years; leading sources (countries) of imports

B. By Country

Vital statistics: population, climate, etc.

Major business cities and regions

Total imports in recent years

Active competitors and market shares

Local competition

Political and economic background

Import duties and taxes

Development plans

Government budgets

Foreign aid

Table 2. Tactical Intelligence Checklist

A. Agents Handling Your Type of Product at National, Provincial, and Local Levels

Names and addresses

Annual sales

Products (manufacturers) represented

Market share

Locations (branches, showrooms, stores)

Owners and managing directors

Sales managers

Key or outstanding sales personnel

Personal data on directors, sales executives, and salespeople

Selling terms and conditions

Favored promotion schemes

B. Submarkets within the Country

Provinces, cities, municipalities, outlying territories

Most active, competitive submarkets; dominant local firms

Submarkets ignored by the competition; possible reasons; characteristics; accessibility

C. End Users (Including Government)

Leading organizations

Purchasing procedures

Persons in charge

Buyers

Sources of supply; favored manufacturers and local firms

Budgets

D. Special Projects

Organizations in charge

Source and size of funds

Shopping list

Consultants and contractors

Persons in charge of specifications and purchasing

Favored sources of supply; manufacturers and local firms

E. Promotion Media—Scope and Costs

Newspapers and magazines

Radio and TV

Direct mail facilities

Trade fairs

Outdoor advertising

Special events sponsored by your country's government

to contact their key people, learn who they really are, their backgrounds and training, personality traits, what makes them good or bad. The same goes for the people in charge of end user organizations and special projects.

When you try to learn about the competition, the magic word, once again, is *people*. Marketing battles are won or lost by men and women. Intelligence on the competition has a double edge: It can quickly lead to countermeasures at the local level, and it can help you figure out world-

Table 3. Competition Intelligence Checklist

A. At the International Level

President or managing director.

Person in charge of international operations: name; title; years on the job; background; education; previous positions; experience in the field; residence abroad; languages spoken; hobbies; family; frequency of travel.

Other key persons, such as assistant marketing and sales managers, advertising managers, service managers.

Who does most of the traveling and to where?

Source of products/services: in-house or subcontracted; licensees/joint ventures in other countries.

International marketing network: countries where active; overseas branch offices and/or field sales offices; overseas agents.

Type of marketing organization: direct sales force, licensees, joint ventures, importing wholesalers, distributors, retailers, commission agents.

Regional managers and salespeople: names, home bases, background, languages, nationality, prior experience in the field, previous employment, how long in present job/location, other professional and personal data.

Participation in major international trade shows.

Main features of product, including price, models, etc.

Is product especially designed for international markets?

Countries where the m/s* has a leading market share.

Major contract awards or sales.

Countries where the m/s is weak or absent.

Promotional material: brochures, catalogs, newsletters, sales manuals; languages and formats.

International sales meetings: how often and where?

B. Country by Country

Method of covering the target country: branch offices, resident sales personnel, agents, etc.

Agents, licensees, or joint venture partners: where are they located; do they cover the entire country or submarkets; how long representing the same m/s; who's who in these organizations.

Estimate of agents' satisfaction or dissatisfaction with the m/s; reasons.

Person responsible for the country: full-time resident field manager or salesperson; background, including professional and personal data; how many years in the country, home base, etc.

Additional territory covered by the same person: which countries; frequency and extent of travel.

Frequency and length of visits to target country.

Estimate of autonomy and initiative of field/local m/s personnel.

Submarkets where the m/s is dominant.

Major national or submarket contracts and sales.

Submarkets where inactive or weak.

End users who favor the product.

Favored local promotion schemes.

Participation in local promotion.

Estimate of reasons for success or failure in the target country and its submarkets.

(*) m/s = manufacturer/supplier.

wide marketing patterns, promotion schemes, and long-range policies of your competition.

Table 3 is a checklist of what you should learn about competitors. Emphasize personal information on key people.

A continuing evaluation of the competition reveals:

1. Markets where the competition is strong. It could be tough and costly for you to move into them.

2. Markets where the competition is weak or absent. Some could be attractive targets for you.

3. Marketing techniques which worked or failed. Compare with your own.

4. The competition's most talented marketing executives and salespeople, their spheres of action.

Know Your Suppliers

If you are an agent, your intelligence requirements are the same, in terms of your territory. There is an additional, important target: *suppliers.*

Unless you are interested in a one-shot deal, you should learn all you can about a supplier before negotiating an agreement. The sloppy way to contact suppliers is when a hot deal pops up and you dash off telexes asking for immediate quotations and exclusivity. This happens in booming markets, as in Saudi Arabia in the 1970s and early 1980s. Good and lasting contacts are seldom made this way. Why should the person at the other end listen to your story? Other agents in your country are probably trying to get the same line. The company may already have a local agent. Experienced firms won't give you an exclusive franchise overnight. The larger the supplier, the less excitement your frantic appeals will generate.

Early in the game you should find out if the supplier you are after is seriously interested in your country or territory. If you are an agent in a relatively small country, you may find that the supplier you contact has targeted three big markets elsewhere and has no time for yours. A persistent and convincing approach on your part may indeed convince the supplier to open up your market—large or small. Or you may learn not to waste time with the particular firm.

The smart way, whatever your motivation and situation, is to do your homework early. Table 4 is a short checklist of the information you should collect and update at all times, on top of the strategic, tactical, and competitive intelligence you need from within your own territory.

If you seek and evaluate manufacturers and suppliers when there is no immediate rush, you will end up with stronger agreements than when you try to do a last-minute job of it.

Links and Sources

The people who use market intelligence—sales forces and decision-making executives—don't always know what information they need. The initiative of those who gather and evaluate data has a lot to do with the quality of the intelligence that is eventually passed on to its users.

Conventional intelligence includes: government trade publications and reports; association and industry directories; industry bulletins, newsletters, and magazines; business newspapers and weekly magazines; the daily press; classified telephone directories; trade fair directories; atlases, world almanacs, and encyclopedias; *Who's Who* directories; and directories of consulting organizations.

Table 4. Special Intelligence Checklist for Agents

Countries producing products of interest

Imports from each for the last few years

Names and addresses of manufacturers/suppliers (m/s)

Persons in charge of international marketing, including professional and personal background, knowledge of country and language

Favored marketing system: exclusive or nonexclusive; branches or local agents; resident or visiting field managers and other sales people

Description of product line, including prices, catalogs, brochures, samples of advertising

Estimate of success of product line and m/s in other countries in immediate region

Type of marketing setup most likely to appeal to the m/s, including intelligence, personnel, promotion, service, contact with key end users, noncompeting lines carried

Do you have a library? If not, set one up right away, no matter how small. Stock it with all possible conventional intelligence publications, including competitors' catalogs.

Collecting this information in the United States means contacting the nearest district office of the International Trade Administration (U.S. Department of Commerce), state organizations, and industry associations. You should also make frequent use of the Library of Congress, local and university libraries (particularly the libraries of business schools), the libraries of foreign chambers of commerce and of at least the major embassies and consulates of foreign countries.

The variety and quantity of information readily available, if you know where to look, is overwhelming. One of the best and most comprehensive listings of intelligence information sources is *Competitor Intelligence*, by Leonard Fuld (John Wiley & Sons, Inc., New York, 1985). It contains extensive listings of sources, not only in the United States but in most countries around the world.

You should gather these types of intelligence particularly in the countries where your competitors are located, and in your priority markets. Visit the commercial libraries of their embassies and consulates regularly, and you will be able to identify dozens of useful sources.

Just because all this information is readily available and often free, don't assume that it is worthless. The trick lies in using it. Five international marketing managers may read and analyze the same report. Four of them file the information away; they don't know what else to do with it. The fifth one puts it to work, makes it pay off.

Intelligence involves the smart use of links and sources. In the next two chapters we will see how you can use sources in priority countries and on the competition's own home ground. To find them you need links. Whether you are a manufacturer, a supplier, or an agent, you may already have useful links within your organization that you are not aware of. Look around you. Do you know where they are? How to cultivate and use them?

3
In-House Links

Jacques Lafleur, export manager for a Montreal supplier of computer peripherals, has heard rumors that his agent in Thailand may have taken on a competitor's line. Thailand is a good market for Jacques but he cannot squeeze in a special trip to Bangkok for several months. Still, he must check out the rumors right away.

He can phone or telex the agent, but without any facts Jacques will not be leading from a position of strength. Someone must visit the agent's showroom and see what is happening. Only then, with facts at his fingertips, will Jacques be able to come up with an aggressive plan of attack.

He calls in his assistant bookkeeper, Thanom Surapraphant, a young immigrant who had arrived from Thailand two years before.

"Your brother Kanchit still teaching at Chulalongkorn University?" Jacques asks, after looking up Thanom's file.

"Yes. He teaches economics. I just got a letter from him."

"I can use his help," Jacques says. He explains the situation. "Do you think Kanchit can drop into these people's showroom as a customer and find out what's going on? I'll give you a list of questions he should ask."

"I'm sure he will be happy to do it."

"I'll pay him $200. I don't need a fancy report. Just straight answers. Can you telex him?"

"No problem. We know the telex operator at one of the hotels in Bangkok."

Five days later Kanchit comes through with the answers. The rumors are true. Jacques mails him two $100 bills in separate envelopes, stuffed inside company brochures. Now he can go on the attack. He telexes the agent for an explanation, giving him straight facts to show he knows what's happening. He also prepares a contingency plan to reopen contact with another Bangkok firm which had wanted the line earlier.

Thanom is happy; his goodwill and cooperative attitude toward the company can do him no harm. Kanchit picks up as much money as he regularly earns in two weeks. Perhaps Lafleur will have another assignment for him soon.

This basic and direct contact gives Jacques the information he needs, quickly and cheaply. Without Kanchit's report the Bangkok problem could have dragged on unnoticed until Jacques' next visit to Bangkok months later, costing the company thousands of dollars in lost business. Now he can pressure his agent right away, switch to another one if needed, cut his losses, and rebuild sales.

Jacques is a tactical-minded export manager who knows the value of local sources and that sound intelligence involves *street-level chores*—what Kanchit did in Bangkok. Intelligence from sources like Kanchit is real and tangible. The secret is to find Kanchits. Jacques Lafleur has friends around the world, but not all can or will carry out the type of assignment Jacques gave Kanchit. Some would be insulted if Jacques offered them money.

For some intelligence, the alternative to sources like Kanchit is to use government channels or consultants. If you, a U.S. manufacturer, want to assess a distributor in Bangkok, you can submit a request to the nearest field office of the Department of Commerce. But it will take weeks for the request to reach the commercial officer at the U.S. embassy in Thailand, and more weeks before a report gets back to you. Another problem: Government information is usually in the public domain, and may appear in trade publications and other reports read by competitors.

A consultant will probably subcontract to a firm in Thailand. This can eventually cost you thousands of dollars. In either case, government or consultant, *the actual legwork in Thailand will be done by someone like Kanchit,* except that the information is embellished with opinions, statistics, charts, projections, and tables you may not need, all of which will delay your getting a final report.

Jacques Lafleur chose the quickest, cheapest, and most practical approach.

The way to outside sources like Kanchit is through personal links. The best and least expensive are in-house people—including employees like Thanom Surapraphant.

The first step in setting up your own intelligence service is to check out *every executive and employee in your company who has contact with people in other countries.* You may have more in-house links with sources abroad than you think, not only in offices but in every department of your company, including production—valuable people right under your nose. How long have you been ignoring them? Seek links also in all of your branch and regional offices abroad.

If you are an agent, your need for in-house links is just as pressing. Anybody in your organization with personal contacts in the countries where your suppliers are located can make a useful contribution to your business.

Use in-house links. Start looking for them today. Through them you can get a lot of practical intelligence at negligible cost.

Active In-House Links

International executives, field managers, salespeople, and marketing staff in your company and overseas offices are the best links. They are close to the operation and (in most cases) have experience in dealing with people abroad. Also important are executives in other departments—including accounting, production, advertising, and promotion—who may on occasion travel abroad.

Anybody who travels abroad on business can find and cultivate sources and bring back intelligence from each trip. Unfortunately too often your people may set out on trips without knowing or being told what to look for.

Every traveler, particularly field managers and salespeople, should be briefed meticulously at the start of a trip. Briefing must be specific. Here are some important points to remember:

1. Nobody should leave without a shopping list of desirable intelligence tailored to the person's itinerary, experience, position, and contacts abroad.

2. Avoid overlapping between persons traveling to the same country or event. For instance, coordinate the people going to a trade fair or convention. How many are going? For what purpose? What important sources or contacts does each person have? Who should try to ferret out information about this or that competitor? What type of information?

3. Be realistic about how much time the traveler will have for intelligence. Most business travelers are always in a rush. Better cover two countries thoroughly than try to cram six into a short schedule.

4. Travelers should be in full control of their comings and goings. Falling into the clutches of an agent is a guarantee that you will be wined and dined and will see only what makes the agent look good. If your visit is intended mainly to gather intelligence, don't announce the exact date of your arrival to agents.

The same happens, in reverse, to agents who take business trips to the countries where their suppliers are located. A supplier who is afraid you will start talking to the competition will do everything possible to keep you fully occupied and entertained during your visit.

5. Allow enough time for briefing. If you are like most executives, you spend the last day before a trip abroad in a frenzy of stuffing unread papers into an attache case and giving repetitive and unnecessary instructions to assistants, leaving no time left for a briefing.

Before the briefing, the intelligence manager should be thoroughly prepared with answers to a few basic questions (see suggested list in Table 5),

Table 5. Prebriefing Questions

How much time will the traveler spend abroad?

Cities to be visited?

Regular business trip or special event?

Purpose of trip?

Which sources in each city should be contacted?

Does the traveler know them?

Special instructions or assignments to sources?

New source to be contacted?

Suggestions on how to cultivate existing sources?

Can trip improve knowledge of competition?

What intelligence gaps (market or competition) can be filled?

Should traveler check or verify data already on file?

Need any specific local publications or reports?

---

so that the briefing itself can be devoted entirely to discussing the traveler's intelligence shopping list.

A similar checklist can be used by someone traveling abroad on behalf of an agent. In addition to contacting sources of information, the traveler probably will also include visits to suppliers and manufacturers the agent may want to do business with in the future.

Intelligence shopping lists should be short. *The more questions you ask, the more you will discourage the traveler.* With time always at a premium, try for a few good answers. The traveler is only a link to one or more sources. The main purpose of his or her trip is to sell or conduct other business, *not* to gather intelligence. Salespersons have calls to make and cannot afford much time to dig around for market information.

Shopping list aside, encourage travelers to use their own imagination and initiative, to keep their eyes and ears open to anything that could be useful.

Other In-House Links: People with Connections

"Good connections" usually implies influential big shots who can steer business your way. In intelligence, prestige and position are not always as important as the ability to deliver functional information. Often this can be done better by working-level people than by top brass. Don't underestimate intelligence which does not come from executives or international marketing people.

How widely throughout your company should you seek links? Obviously if you have a work force of 35,000 people in offices and factories, you won't be able to canvass them one by one. You can confine your efforts to personnel in the international marketing department and supporting departments, and remind everybody else, through company newspapers and internal bulletins, of your interest in foreign contacts.

Who in your company is likely to have connections abroad? People with relatives and friends in other countries are the most obvious. In virtually every company in the United States, Australia, Canada, Argentina, Brazil, and Israel, numbers of employees have parents or grandparents who migrated from other countries. There are also many descendants of immigrants in West Germany, France, and the United Kingdom.

Streams of Irish, German, English, Dutch, Swedish, Norwegian, Italian, Austro-Hungarian, Bulgarian, Greek, Russian, Chinese, and Japanese people have migrated to the United States since the end of the nineteenth century. Recently there has been an invasion from Latin America, the Middle East, and Southeast Asia. Since 1960 the largest numbers of immigrants to the United States have come from the West Indies, Mexico, and the Philippines. There were also huge contingents from South Korea, China, India, and Vietnam. Three hundred thousand Asian immigrants arrived in 1984 alone.

These massive migrations have created in the United States a vast and intricate web of personal connections reaching every country in the world. Few companies in international marketing are taking advantage of it.

Similar far-flung webs extend from Canada, Australia, the United Kingdom, and France. Migration to Europe has originated mainly in Africa, the Middle East, south and southeast Asia. Hundreds of thousands of people have moved from Portugal, Spain, Greece, Yugoslavia, and Turkey to the northern European countries.

Companies in countries favored with expanding immigration have access to a vast storehouse of intelligence links with sources all over the world. Japanese companies, invariably staffed entirely by Japanese, lack the advantage of this valuable asset. However, subsidiaries of Japanese companies in the United States and Western Europe inevitably do have in-house links to sources in other markets. Look for links in all offices, not just back home.

Relatives in the country of origin are not always useful intelligence sources. They may live in rural areas. They may be too old. They may be poorly educated. They may not have time for occasional extra work.

The best links are those who know working people—office workers, salespeople, teachers, government officials, scientists, technicians, engineers, researchers, lawyers, accountants, and junior executives—preferably in cities where there is ample and fairly easy access to information.

You may do better with links who are new immigrants than with second- and third-generation children of immigrants. New arrivals are still close to friends and family "back home." They maintain the language and may receive newspapers and magazines regularly. Friends and relatives who may themselves be eager to migrate will be particularly willing to cooperate with companies which might later offer them jobs.

Friends back home may be more useful than family. People easily move away from families, develop a world of their own with others of similar interests, education, and background. An Indian mechanical engineer will have better connections among engineers and government officials in Bombay, where he or she studied and worked, than in the small village in the Punjab where he or she was born.

Employees who receive newspapers and other publications from abroad can be useful. Newspapers carry news of local companies, arrivals of executives from other countries, development projects, contract awards, appointments and promotions of business and government leaders, social receptions, and plenty of other information which can help you keep track of opportunities, trends, the whereabouts of your competition, and agency appointments.

Newspaper advertising reveals a lot about what your competition and your local agents are doing. I buy and scan newspapers everywhere I go, even when I cannot read the language. Ads are particularly instructive. *Local newspapers are the most important single source of market intelligence.* Any information about the types of people your competitors are hiring will give you valuable clues about their priority markets and overall expansion.

The continuing movement of migrants also favors agents. In virtually every company in the Middle East, Asia, Latin America, and parts of Africa, you will find employees with friends or relatives who have emigrated to the United States, Australia, Canada, France, the United Kingdom, West Germany, or other European countries.

There may be other employees in your company with connections abroad. Tens of thousands of secondary school and university students are in exchange programs throughout the world. Employees who give exchange students room and board may not realize that they are excellent potential sources which can be cultivated before they return to their countries. Exchange students can be taken on tours of your factories and offices, introduced to international marketing people, given product demonstrations, loaded up with catalogs, briefed on possible intelligence assignments.

Other useful links are diplomats, military officers, and teachers who have served abroad for any length of time. You may not have any among your staff, but look for employees who may know some.

Employees who travel abroad on their own, not on company business, can bring back useful information. Travel is now within reach of almost everybody. Who in your company went abroad last summer? Where did they go? How long did they stay? What did they see? Whom did they meet? Where did they shop?

Most vacationers go in groups, seldom meet anybody other than tour guides, hotel receptionists, waiters, bellboys, and cabdrivers. But these packaged explorers still spend endless hours drifting in and out of shops and can be useful in picking up specific basic information—if they know what to look for. People who don't travel in groups obviously have a great deal of flexibility and could be more valuable.

The least you can ask a traveler to do is buy and mail you copies of the latest classified telephone directories of the cities visited. They are among the best sources of information on major end users such as government agencies, which agents are representing your competition, the number of retail outlets. Classified phone directories should be part of your intelligence library.

In countries where companies employ large number of expatriates—the notable examples are the oil-producing countries of the Middle East—agents have a unique opportunity to enlist the services of personnel who go abroad on annual leave.

What to Expect from In-House Links

Encourage employees to contribute intelligence from any country. If you are the intelligence manager, don't even overlook information from a low-priority market; it may be useful when your company is ready to move into it.

If your priority targets include some of the world's top markets, such as most West European countries, the United States, Canada, and Japan, take advantage of every possible link your employees may have. You need all the information and all the help you can get.

Briefing in-house links who are not involved in marketing is a fishing expedition. For a start, ask them to send their friends and relatives company and product catalogs, and possibly a general list of the information you would be interested in. The list can be based on one of the tables in Chapter 2.

This casual approach is also good public relations and promotion. But make sure you know who the sources are and that they may be at least somewhat useful. Don't let the links become too involved; they have their regular jobs to do, and you will be wise to take as little of their time as possible.

Keep the value of sources in perspective. Don't expect miracles but be prepared for pleasant surprises.

A Swiss manufacturer of electronic measuring instruments was about to participate in a commercial trade fair in China for the first time. Corinne Metral, the export manager, spread the word within the company that she would like to talk to anybody who had possible personal contacts in China, no matter how tenuous. A young technician from the engineering department turned up. "My brother is a professor of biology," the technician said. "He was in China last year on a lecture tour of several universities."

Corinne met the brother and got the names of three Chinese professors who had kept in touch with him. Through them Corinne reached other academics and professionals who later proved valuable in introducing the product and creating the company's first sales in China.

This type of personal connection is priceless. Look around you. You may be overlooking unique opportunities to improve your position in priority markets through in-house links.

Table 6 gives you an idea of what to ask in-house links about their contacts abroad. The list is simple and flexible enough to cover also contacts with exchange students and other visitors from abroad.

The checklist should be brief. The more details you try to gather, the greater the risk of burying legitimate intelligence under piles of useless verbiage.

Briefing people about to go on vacation should also be low-key. Let them know that you will welcome any information that relates to the company and its product. You may give someone a clear assignment that takes little time and effort, such as bringing back catalogs of competitive products, copies of newspaper ads, or walking into a retail store and checking

Table 6. Basic Facts on Sources in Other Countries

Name of contact.

Address.

Age.

Education and background.

Job or profession.

Position.

Does the person travel within the country? Abroad?

Friend or relative?

When and how did you meet?

Do you keep in touch regularly? Correspond?

Does contact send you newspapers and other publications?

Do you plan to go "back home" soon? When?

prices of merchandise on display—perhaps even checking out your agent, as Kanchit did for Jacques Lafleur.

If you are an agent, a typical assignment to give a vacationing employee is to visit the offices or showrooms of suppliers in whose products you may be interested.

Debriefing

Useful intelligence can be squeezed out of executives and employees who have been abroad if you debrief them immediately after they come back. Intelligence is wasted when you don't systematically and thoroughly question everybody who has been abroad, even on vacation. The best time to ferret out this information is while it is still fresh in the traveler's mind.

Many travelers don't realize the importance of people met during the trip, are careless with names and addresses, may overlook important conversations unless prodded.

Here are some basic principles of debriefing:

1. Everybody should be debriefed, including the company's president, other executives, directors, officers, field managers, and salespeople. Also agents and business visitors from abroad, whether or not connected with the company.

2. Don't rush it. Debriefing can last minutes or hours. Returning executives and *anybody* in international marketing should be thoroughly debriefed, no matter how long it takes. Others may be debriefed in minutes, particularly when they were not given specific assignments.

3. Don't ask for written reports. They take time and effort, and few people can write concisely. Busy executives and salespeople will welcome the time saved.

4. Debrief people in their offices or work stations. Make the process as painless as possible. Not everybody takes kindly to inquisitors. If important, take the person to lunch.

5. Debriefing visitors not connected with the company calls for tact. The person has no reason to give you information. You, the intelligence officer, should adopt an unobtrusive role, such as being included as one of the guests at a luncheon or dinner for the visitor.

In large companies it may be impossible to personally debrief everybody who has contact with people abroad. Preliminary screening may be necessary, such as talking only to people with links in priority markets.

Debriefing executives and international marketing people should not be limited to the shopping list you gave the traveler at the start of the trip. Try to bring out other information, such as the names of people met in airplanes or at social occasions, their affiliations, subjects discussed.

Debriefing company employees who were not given intelligence assignments is a matter of finding out where the person went, and names and addresses of people met.

Debriefing visitors from abroad consists mainly of asking discreet questions about their countries, local conditions, opinions.

Briefing and debriefing company executives and employees is easier, more effective, and better understood when all personnel have been trained in the importance of market intelligence and the basic techniques of gathering useful information.

Are In-House Links Useful?

Trace the origins of some of your company's major sales, and you will find that many started with a casual comment picked up during a conversation, a notice read in a newspaper, or information volunteered by a visitor.

In-house links are one more way to keep yourself informed. Don't overlook them. You never know enough about markets and competition. You never know if you are missing an opportunity. Business runs on personal connections. Not all of them have to be high-level, high-power contacts.

4

Thinktanks and
Street-Level Sources

Digging for intelligence means finding sources, telling them what you want, and *listening to what they tell you*. Not every head office likes to listen. Does yours?

In 1951 I was a rookie salesman in New York City for a Swedish manufacturer of calculating machines. That was when bulky machines with 100 or more keys were beginning to give way to the newer 10-key version. Underwood, Victor, Olivetti, and other manufacturers were promoting the keyboard which eventually became a worldwide standard for office machines and pushbutton telephones. The firm I worked for had other ideas: the only rational and functional 10-key keyboard, they insisted, was their own, with the keys laid out in two parallel rows. The proof of the pudding, I was told, was that the company dominated most markets around the world. The United States would be the next target.

Lugging calculating machines around in those days was no picnic. Some models weighed 50 pounds. Competition was tough. Prospective buyers, spoiled by offers of free demonstrations, kept and used machines for days before deciding whether to buy or not.

I was one of six salespeople in the office. Week after week we pounded the sidewalks of Manhattan carrying our demonstrators. Sales were as rare as trees in a desert. In addition to finding legitimate prospects, we had to convince them that our machines were as good as any made in the United States. In those days, "Buy American" was the unshakable credo of most office managers we approached. But the real problem was our different two-row keyboard, which no other manufacturer had chosen to adopt.

We sent dozens of detailed and documented reports to Stockholm about this hopeless, suicidal attack against overwhelming odds. Stockholm was unshakable: rational studies by objective scientists at leading Swedish institutes had proved that the two-row keyboard was superior. It was up to us to "educate the public" and quit griping. Eventually, reluctantly, Stockholm listened. In the meantime, many years had been wasted.

Where to Set up Sources

A tight, well-run, productive intelligence service concentrates its resources rather than dispersing them worldwide, particularly if the targets include large, major markets. The principle is the same for large and small firms. The difference is one of resources.

Where should you seek and plant sources?

1. *As close as possible to your competitors—even inside their operations.* There are legitimate, above-board ways of doing this.

2. *In markets where you are already strong.* You have already spent time, money, and human resources to set foot in them. Stay ahead of the game!

3. *In newly targeted markets.* Your strategic assessment done, you now need to quickly build up local sources to help you develop sales.

If you are an agent, apply the same principles to your own territory.

Inside the Competition

The least you should know about the competition, is outlined in Table 3 (Chapter 2). What sources do you need?

1. *Your own marketing executives and salespeople.* They should identify, meet, and try to shadow their *counterparts* in the competition. Check the key players in the opposition, at all levels. If you don't know the names of a competitor's international marketing manager, field managers, and salespeople, pick up the phone and find out. The easiest way is to call the company directly. If this doesn't work, check with one of your competitor's agents. Follow the same approach to learn where the field managers and salespeople are stationed. Ask for their addresses. This will give you a quick picture of the competitor's key markets and bases.

Talking to a competitor can be revealing. Sharing interests and experiences makes it easier for people—even competitors—to loosen up with each other. What better way for two salespeople to hit it off than by griping about unbending bosses? Or by sharing stories about unique adventures in distant lands?

Why should competitors talk to you? For any number of reasons. Because they may think they are sitting on top of the world and consider you as a harmless upstart. Because it pays to make friends; someday they may come to you for a job. *Because people would rather talk than listen.* Most of all because people like to brag about themselves—their achievements, know-how, experience—and their companies.

In international marketing it is easier to find a show-off than a diplomat. Get people to talk and you will pick up all sorts of information. Of course, talking to a competitor also makes you vulnerable. But if you take the initiative and remember a few simple rules which we will discuss in the chapter on training, you can keep a tight rein on what you give away. You may disclose an item or two, but will the other person remember it the next morning? And use it? Probably not.

Where do you meet competitors? Take the bull by the horns—start with their home and field offices. Phoning for an appointment and dropping in for a chat is unorthodox; it will certainly shake up a competitor and give you the advantage of surprise.

Trade fairs and conventions are perfect places to meet competitors. Don't waste these opportunities. Don't avoid personal contact, as most salespeople do, preferring instead to pick up literature as unobtrusively as possible. Train your sales people to be realistic and aggressive, to walk up to competitors' booths and introduce themselves. This can lead to many fruitful and friendly contacts.

If you are an agent, your immediate competitors are other agents in your city or country. You probably meet them frequently at association gatherings or socially. If not, make a point of improving your contacts with them.

2. *Your agents.*   They will not tell you everything they learn, but they have ample opportunities to meet your competitors' marketing executives and salespeople. Competitors who are not always trying to woo a good agent away from you are not doing their job, unless your agent is too weak to be attractive to them. Either way, this tells you something about a competitor.

Eager competitors will disclose to a desirable agent priceless information about their marketing policies, discount structure, promotion schemes, the people in charge of marketing, and their success in other markets—all as part of their sales pitch. An alert agent can take advantage of this to ask questions. The more desirable the agent, the easier it is to get answers. Your job, if you are the intelligence manager for an international supplier, is to keep after your agents to tell you what they know.

If you are an agent, on the other hand, your concern is always how to achieve a happy balance between how much you know and how much you tell the suppliers you represent. The more contact you have with your suppliers' competitors, the more you learn about their operations, the stronger your position will be when you deal with your suppliers or when you decide to shift to another line.

3. *Consultants.*   They are excellent sources if pointed in the right direction and given clear instructions. They know a lot of people. They can

move about freely, have legitimate reasons to visit your competitors and ask questions as part of research projects, such as evaluating the local market for a specific product. A bit transparent? Perhaps. But consultants do have to keep up with market developments. Their research does not necessarily have to be for immediate clients.

Businesspeople usually like to talk to consultants. In dozens of research assignments around the world since the early 1960s, I never failed to run into executives eager to prove me wrong. Give businesspeople a chance to be all-knowing experts. Imply that other firms are doing better and you may trigger a gush of facts, figures, and opinions. Nobody wants to be labeled a loser. In the process, the consultant picks up valuable information about other competitors. Give consultants ongoing assignments to keep track of specific competitors.

Where do you find consultants? Let's say your firm in the United States wants to check out a competitor in Milan. You ask the commercial officer at the U.S. consulate in Milan if any Italian consultants have recently done any research in your field. For good measure, you also check with the Italian desk at the U.S. Department of Commerce (DOC) in Washington. If DOC is planning a special promotion in Italy, such as a show at the Milan Trade Center, a catalog exhibition, or a trade mission, an independent U.S. consultant may have prepared a feasibility study under contract to DOC.

You contact the Italian and the U.S. consultants, find out how much they know and whether you can use their services to pick up information about your competitor. The Italian consultant in particular could become a useful link for future assignments.

Local agents can also make excellent use of consultants in evaluating local projects and opportunities, also abroad, to scout for new lines and suppliers.

4. *Association officials.* Join the professional and industrial associations your competitors belong to. If some of your toughest competitors are located in other countries, find out which associations in those countries they belong to, and try to join them as well.

Association membership gives you access to bulletins, newsletters, seminars, conferences, and lectures. An association opens opportunities to meet competitors personally.

Association officials can tell you a lot about competitors—who's who, sales volume, lists of agents abroad. This data is probably on file and available to anybody who cares to look it up.

Who should be your link with association officials? In your own country this should be handled by the international marketing manager. Abroad, it should be someone in the country itself, such as a field manager or salesperson, who can attend meetings and call on officials regularly.

5. *Travel agents.* You can spot your competitors' priority targets by tracing the travels of their international salespeople around the world. This also tells you which markets are being ignored, and adds to your knowledge of competitors' strategies and tactics. The travel agent who handles a competitor's account can be a very valuable source.

Using travel agents as sources takes time, patience, and tact. After a travel agent has been cultivated, contact can be kept easily through frequent phone calls.

Cultivating the travel sector can be equally rewarding if you are a local agent. You can keep track of the travels abroad of your local competitors. You can monitor the comings and goings of visiting field managers and salespeople who work for firms that compete with your suppliers. The information is valuable to them and tells you which other manufacturers are taking an active interest in your market.

6. *Trade publication reporters and editors.* Find out which trade magazines, newsletters, and bulletins are published in the countries of your competitors, meet their editors and call on them whenever you visit the country. They will have plenty of information on file about your competitors, and probably know many of their marketing executives personally.

In return, they will welcome information about your company and product. Put them on your mailing list for press releases, send them catalogs, and buy advertising space if you can afford it.

Cultivate local newspapers, as well. If any articles have been written about a competitor, the reporter who wrote the story would be an interesting person to meet.

7. *Government sources.* Not all of the information gathered by embassy commercial officers comes out in official reports. Government reports may be impersonal, but the officers responsible for compiling them may themselves be in touch with key executives in the industry. Don't write them off as desk-bound bureaucrats!

Country by Country

To gather intelligence in priority markets, outside sources are your best bet. In most countries you may need them only sporadically for specific, street-level jobs. In major markets you will need them often. Outside sources should gather the types of intelligence spelled out in the tables in Chapter 2. There are many ways they can get the job done. Intelligence-conscious local agents can follow the same routes to develop this information for their own purposes.

1. *Collect local documentation.* Start with local classified telephone directories. You can ask your source to scan them and send you copies of the pages of interest to you, but it would be better for you to have the entire publication and browse through it yourself. You will uncover a lot of information you had not thought of looking up in the first place.

Make a list of the local publications you would like to receive regularly. (Your agents may do it, but don't count on it.) Include government trade statistics, tax regulations, bulletins and newsletters from professional groups and associations, important articles from daily newspapers, industry directories, and any other types of documentation which are readily available. This simple job requires no special skills and takes little time. The important thing is to do it regularly.

In major markets you can get trade information by subscription. This leaves your sources free to scan the daily press and other publications that would take too much of your time to review every day.

2. *Keep tabs on the competition.* Competing sales forces are made up of in-country sales managers, salespeople, agents, licensees, or joint-venture partners. You need to keep tabs on them to find out where they are active, what tactics they may be using, and to identify their star performers.

Which levels of the local competition are important to you? It depends on your product. If your line is sophisticated medical instruments sold directly to end users, you need sources to develop contacts with the competition's salespeople. If your line is office stationery, cultivating salespeople who stand behind counters in retail stores is not essential. You should develop links with the leading importers and wholesalers in the country, and with the salespeople who cover their retail outlets.

When you track the competition, you cannot give your sources exact instructions. It is not like asking someone to visit five department stores and check the price of a bottle of shampoo. Sources working on the competition have to be resourceful, tactful, discreet, and imaginative. You must evaluate and qualify them carefully.

Basic and indispensable competitor information you should receive quickly and regularly includes clippings of all newspaper advertising—on products, special sales, and promotions—press releases, and help-wanted notices by competitors' agents.

How does a local source follow the comings and goings, failures and successes of competitors? Say you are a university professor in Indonesia with free time for outside work. You are a source for a U.S. tractor manufacturer who wants to keep up with the activities of all the Indonesian agents in the tractor business, and their top salespeople. You make a list of the organizations the salespeople are likely to call on frequently—the Ministry of Agriculture, agricultural colleges, farmers' cooperatives, farm equipment distributors and dealers. You find out if the salespeople belong to any associations, business and sports clubs.

Next, you take inventory of the people you know in these organizations, and you start calling on them for help. Before long you are bound to meet some of the competition's salespeople and learn about their movements.

Crossing the line between business and friendship can cause problems. Say you contrive to meet Theo Soemarko, salesman for a Japanese manufacturer. You become friends, meet occasionally for dinner or drinks. Theo begins to drop bits of information about his travels within Indonesia, his product, his customers, and projects. The U.S. manufacturer is delighted, but you have a problem. Should you tell Theo what you are up to?

There's no easy answer. No two situations are ever alike. Telling Theo will not necessarily kill the contact or the friendship. Theo could in fact be interested. Suppose he welcomes the chance to access your U.S. manufacturer? Suppose he is not happy with his job and wants to make a switch?

3. *Cultivate VIPs.* The purpose of international marketing is to sell. In major markets learn all you can about projects and opportunities, and *the people who are influential in recommending or buying your product.* Sources who can get you this information are worth their weight in gold.

VIPs are fairly easy to spot and contact. A source's simplest and most direct approach is to play the role of market researcher for an international supplier. The VIP will probably welcome the contact as a chance to learn more about product, specifications, prices, and other information which comes in handy when preparing budgets and projects.

If your company produces language laboratories, for instance, the VIPs to pursue are the top officials, purchasing agents, and foreign language advisors in ministries of education; presidents and heads of the language departments of all universities; directors of regional and local educational authorities; headmasters of major private schools and language academies; in-house language training directors in big corporations.

Your local agents may be trying to sell the same VIPs. No matter. Selling and gathering intelligence are distinct tasks. Besides, your agents may not be sending you enough information. Ask yourself, are you getting early word on important projects, before everybody else has learned about them? Do you have a reasonable list of VIPs in the country? You probably can use outside sources to fill many gaps in your VIP intelligence.

4. *Shop for prices, promotions, discounts, terms.* Pricing consumer products can be a simple matter of walking into a retail store, asking a few questions, and noting how products are displayed and positioned. Pricing sophisticated instrumentation may require discreet contact with purchasing personnel in major end-user organizations.

Information on promotions can be easily gathered from newspaper and professional journal advertising, TV commercials, and other media. Finding out about discounts and terms may take a bit of digging, but a source with access to retailers and end users should manage without serious problems.

These assignments are clear-cut and specific. The same sources can collect brochures, catalogs, manuals, and copies of newspaper ads.

5. *Utilize commercial libraries.*   Instruct your source to visit local commercial, university, public, embassy, and consulate libraries regularly. Pay special attention to the libraries of any prestigious business schools in the city or country.

Regular visits to embassy and consulate libraries can yield valuable information about the competition. All sorts of useful information flows into embassy libraries and is available to the public—newspapers, journals, catalogs, press releases, directories. Business people, teachers, students, and many others have legitimate reasons for poring over these materials.

One or two visits a month to an embassy or consulate will quickly lead to contact with librarians and commercial officers whose job is to stimulate interest in their countries' products. Eventually, through these contacts an intelligence source can learn much about which of your competitors are active in the country, how often their sales managers and salespeople visit the area, and who they are.

Thinktanks

Not all tactical intelligence is street-level and nitty-gritty. The advice of professionals—a local thinktank—is just as important. If you barge into a country with a know-it-all attitude, you may end up wasting precious time, money, and effort before you begin to learn what the local market is all about.

Your own thinktank in a major, developed market is an absolute necessity. For a U.S. manufacturer to plunge into the Japanese market without first setting up a panel of competent advisors can be suicidal. Unless you are extremely lucky, you can easily make moves that will doom your chances of success in Japan for years to come. The need for advisors applies not only to big markets, but also to the smallest and least sophisticated ones.

How do you set up a local thinktank?

If you intend to crack the Venezuelan market, for instance, find competent individuals in Venezuela to help you develop a practical marketing plan and give you perspectives and ideas which may work in other countries as well. Your Venezuelan thinktank can be made up of university professors, engineers, researchers, government officials, bank executives, and advertising agents, depending on your product and end users. They should not be connected directly with your agent or your own sales force. Their value to you is their objective and professional status.

Make a list of the types of people whose advice could be useful. Don't set up formal panels or committees, or soon you will be mired in needless procedures. Keep thinktanks small and informal. Staying in touch with individual members of the thinktank is the job of the intelligence manager. Write, telex, or phone your thinktanks regularly. When you visit a country, get your thinktank together and thrash out basic but vital questions such as:

"Where is our competition strongest and weakest?"

"How do we promote and advertise our product?"

"Should we set up a local office? Exclusive or nonexclusive agents?"

"Which models will sell best?"

How do you get the most out of a thinktank? By asking questions and *listening*. It may be useful to explain how your company has succeeded (or failed) in other markets. But don't impose on your advisors a set of imported concepts. Learn about the market and its peculiarities. Encourage and stimulate constructive ideas and criticism. Listen!

If you are an agent, you will inevitably be suspicious of any advisory groups set up in your own territory by a supplier. You may resent the possible loss of face, unless you are allowed to participate in the group and perhaps even control it. The supplier may not agree. The only way to avoid unpleasantness is to develop close ties with the supplier, make a professional and systematic effort to promote the product, send the supplier ample market intelligence, and accept any suggestions from a mini-thinktank as constructive criticism. You can even try to preempt the supplier by setting up your own thinktank! The more successful and cooperative you are, the less inclined the supplier will be to shut you out of a thinktank, or even to set one up.

Where to Find Active Sources

You can find sources everywhere. What matters is not their profession or line of work but their access to people or information. First you have to decide what information you need.

In my own experience assessing world markets for educational products, I have learned that I can get a reasonable picture of a market by carefully picking ten knowledgeable persons to interview. The trick is to make sure they are well informed about at least one segment of the market and that they overlap enough to give me a chance to cross-check facts and opinions.

When you build up intelligence sources in a country, decide which segments of the market you want to cover, then find the sources to do the job. Make sure you have enough people to cover all bases. Let us look at some types of sources:

1. *Academics.* Usually good for a variety of assignments, professors and researchers make valuable sources and thinktank members. Frequently they are advisors to government and industry, may be involved in designing projects, drawing up procurement lists, evaluating products and suppliers. They play major roles in Third World countries. Professors in China's top twenty technological and scientific universities will inevitably be involved, in one function or another, in all of the country's priority development projects in the next ten years.

Academics in your field can also be useful to identify and cultivate VIPs and competitors, and to develop regular ties with embassy commercial officers and librarians.

If your product is of interest to universities and other educational institutions, using professors as intelligence sources brings you the added bonus of personal word-of-mouth promotion within the academic community.

In major markets, look for sources in the more prestigious universities, polytechnics, and research institutions. Pay particular attention to well-known graduate schools of business.

2. *University students.* Students can collect documentation, read daily and professional newspapers and journals, get pricing information, cover libraries, pick up catalogs, attend trade fairs, check up on retail stores and showrooms.

Alert, aggressive, inquisitive students can be effective scouts for street-level intelligence. Look for students eager to get into business or whose studies relate to your field. Students who do well as intelligence sources eventually may be candidates for international marketing jobs.

To meet professors and students, call on the deans of university faculties and colleges. Volunteer to give informal talks and seminars about your company and industry, to help bring faculty and students up to date on state-of-the-art developments. Be of service to the academic world and you should soon meet professors and students who can become effective intelligence sources.

Consider also, as an investment toward future sales, sending college graduates to live and work abroad for two or three years. Let them learn languages, cultures, and ways of doing business. Enroll them in local universities and give them basic intelligence assignments. You will gain motivated sources under your control and future international salespeople with grass-roots experience—more weapons against your competition.

3. *Club and association officials.*   You cannot recruit and control these sources, but they can give you a fair amount of free information. Make the rounds of trade associations, business clubs, chambers of commerce, sports and health clubs in the top cities in your priority markets, and you will be sure to run into important end users, VIPs, and competitors.

These sources are passive. They can tell you which members joined recently, who brought visitors from abroad for lunch or dinner, which companies are looking for agents (in a trade or business association), and possibly pass on stimulating rumors about negotiations, projects, and opportunities. They can also point out people you should meet, and arrange introductions.

4. *Nationals living abroad.*   In most markets you may find a resident colony of fellow-nationals—some permanent, some on short assignments. Foreign colonies can be huge. There are 30,000 Japanese in the Washington area, and 50,000 U.S. citizens in Saudi Arabia.

Fellow-nationals abroad are logical intelligence sources. They can collect documentation, carry out pricing assignments, cultivate association and embassy officials, attend trade fairs and special events.

Sources with diplomatic ties—such as spouses and children of embassy personnel—can be effective in contacting commercial officers in the embassies of competing countries, and in getting information on the travels and activities of competitors from your own country. A source who regularly attends high-level diplomatic and government receptions is a plus for any international marketing operation.

You can reach fellow-nationals abroad through embassies. If you are a French manufacturer seeking sources in Argentina, a visit to the French embassy in Buenos Aires will reveal the leading organizations in Argentina to which French people are likely to belong—schools, churches, sports clubs, business clubs, and auxiliary groups, all offering a variety of types of sources to choose from.

5. *Concierges and other hotel services.*   Get to know the concierges of the top three or four hotels in a major city like New Delhi or Bombay, and you will gradually manage to put together a picture of which competitors are visiting the country, when, and how often. This is more easily accomplished in a city where business visitors stay at a few top hotels, more difficult in major cities like London, New York, and Tokyo.

Many hotels have become large, impersonal operations in which the traditional role of the concierge has been dispersed among a number of unimaginative reception clerks usually trained to perform narrow tasks. But the concierge institution is not yet entirely dead.

The most obvious information you can get from a concierge is which competitors are in town, have booked reservations, or have recently been around. In the process you can find out who are your competitors' travel agents back in their home towns.

You cultivate concierges by being respectful and by rewarding them generously for their services. Be specific about which competitors you wish to track. Keep the list short. Soon you will have a good idea of their favorite hotels.

Equally important as sources are secretarial and other business services available in the larger hotels.

6. *Consultants.* Professional consultants will cost you more than informal sources but you should retain them in markets where your sources have left big gaps in your intelligence. Make sure that assignments to consultants are important enough to justify the expense. Don't use consultants to gather documentation that can be picked up by students. Get your money's worth! Use consultants with business, academic, professional, and government connections.

7. *Others.* Any alert, knowledgeable, or well-connected person can qualify as a source. Retirees—government officials, business persons, academics, military officers, and diplomats—can be very useful, particularly if they held top jobs in organizations which are major buyers of your type of product. Their experience and connections can be a straight line to project designers, purchasing agents, decision makers, and other VIPs.

Scouting for sources in priority markets is easier if you don't forget your in-house links—the easiest and cheapest way to start. You may have employees who know teachers, professors, students, government officials, consultants, diplomats, travel agents, hotel personnel, business persons, engineers, lawyers, doctors, and many other people abroad who can make good sources. Or your employees may have friends and relatives who in turn may have access to good sources.

Look at each source as the nucleus of a circle of friends, relatives, and acquaintances that themselves could be useful. Try to socialize with your sources. This will help you expand your contacts.

Briefings and Assignments

Thinktanks don't need much briefing. Their job is to give you opinions and guidance, not to gather day-to-day intelligence. Sources cultivating the competition can only be given general instructions. Most others should work on exact, specific assignments.

To define assignments, you must know the needs of your sales force. A user of intelligence, such as a traveling salesperson, may be hard-put to compile a comprehensive list of facts he or she needs from intelligence. The initiative may have to come from the company's intelligence manager and from field sources.

Sources should not be organized into neat networks and groups. Think-tanks can come together from time to time, but street-level sources are individuals reporting directly either to the company's intelligence manager or to the salesperson responsible for the territory.

No matter how exact the instructions, a source should always be encouraged to show initiative.

Sources should keep these principles in mind:

1. Get the facts.
2. Be specific.
3. Be brief.
4. Report quickly.

Can You Trust a Source?

How can you make sure a source will not offer the same information to a competitor? You can't. Having gone to the trouble of gathering the information, the source may well wonder why he or she might not sell it to *two or three* buyers instead of just one.

Don't let this worry you, unless you have put the source on your payroll as a full-time employee.

A free-lance source may not be able to reach a responsive competitor and present a credible case. If as an intelligence manager you got a letter from a student in Peru offering marketing information for a fee, would you pay? You probably wouldn't even answer!

Your competitors may be the sort who go by the book, quicker to commit $20,000 for a trade fair than $500 for street-level intelligence. They may take forever to convert intelligence into action. Masses of market data are floating around many international marketing offices as for-your-information memos. How often do you see memos *for immediate action*?

Be concerned with gathering, evaluating, and *using* intelligence. Given the same information, your competitors may do nothing—or may do something too late.

There's something else to think about: How important are *you* to the source? What does the source get out of working for you? What long-range incentives will make the source eager to cooperate exclusively with you?

How to Pay Sources

The most obvious reason a source will work with you is money: retainers to consultants, university professors, mini-thinktank members, and others whose work involves some continuity; per-job fees for specific assignments; monthly fees for collecting and sending documentation; gratuities to hotel concierges.

Spell out fees and retainers ahead of time. Watch out for consultants and lawyers who may send you a bill for merely talking to you! I fell into such a situation once in Brunei, innocently under the impression that the solicitor I was talking to was seeing me on behalf of a local bigshot. Avoid long-range or open-ended retainers. Try to keep them on a monthly basis.

The ideal arrangement is when a source sends you intelligence regularly and lets you decide how much it is worth each time. The burden is on you. Pay a niggardly sum, or answer a bit too often that the intelligence is worthless, and you soon will be kissing the source goodbye.

Untold numbers of students around the world are always seeking ways to go abroad to study, particularly to North America and Western Europe. Offer to help a student get an entry visa and admission to a university and you may have a grateful source who seeks no other reward. This source may be short-lived, but will probably be happy to recommend one or more successors.

Some sources may not want or expect payment in cash. Lunches, dinners, or personal gifts may be enough reward. Occasionally people will help you purely out of friendship. Don't get too excited about it, because:

1. You cannot control a source who works for nothing.

2. Free intelligence may be worthless.

3. A source you don't control has no sense of urgency.

Paying a source—with money or in other ways—is essential. Nobody should do something for nothing.

Sources versus Agents

If you operate internationally through agents, developing your own sources can be ticklish.

When your agents in a country are nonexclusive, you don't have much of a problem. You are a French manufacturer, for instance, and have set up thirty-five non-exclusive agents in the United States. They should all be happy if you can feed them information gathered through your own intelligence service.

Suspicion will arise, however, if you deal with an exclusive agent. There is always a nagging fear in the back of an agent's mind that a prized supplier may be out courting a rival. Courtesy is not the only reason agents entertain visiting salespeople. They do it also to control them.

One way to avoid friction with agents is to convince them that any sales-oriented intelligence is quickly passed on to them for action, and that they only stand to gain from your own intelligence gathering.

The flip side is that agents who develop useful market intelligence and do not pass it on to their suppliers will not be earning good points for themselves. Nonexclusive agents are acting prudently and with some sensible logic when they hold back information that may benefit other local agents. (The big-happy-family concept has its limits!) But exclusive agents who value their suppliers should cooperate with and trust them—provided the suppliers do the same. If all intelligence eventually is passed on to the agent, regardless of the source, both sides stand to gain.

Be Alert!

When you travel internationally you come in contact with all sorts of people who can divulge valuable information, usually inadvertently. You meet them casually on airplanes, in cocktail lounges and hotel lobbies, at parties and swimming pools, in any number of places. Most of them like to talk more than they like to listen. Remember this, ask an occasional discreet question, and listen. You will pick up interesting and useful tidbits each time.

Intelligence from all sources—including anything learned from casual encounters—must be quickly funneled into a well-run intelligence service that can digest and put it in the hands of people who will use it.

It does not take special talents, investments, or efforts to set up an efficient intelligence apparatus—even if yours is a minuscule international marketing department.

5

Your Own Intelligence Apparatus

Intelligence and marketing are distinct functions. Their ultimate goals are the same: to promote sales. But intelligence means listening and learning; it requires an inquisitive mind that takes in good news and bad. Marketing carries a specific message, in the form of a product or service, which has to be promoted and sold.

Intelligence is a weapon of marketing.

Marketing is a user of intelligence.

Intelligence has to sell its product to marketing. If both functions are run by the same person, you may have a conflict of interests: much intelligence may be neglected or ignored, and sales will suffer; or too much time may be spent on getting intelligence, not enough on selling.

Because marketing is a full-time job which takes relentless effort and concentration, people in marketing seldom have time to gather or even absorb intelligence. Much of it is set aside to be glanced at when time allows—such as after dinner while watching TV.

International intelligence should be an independent service—no matter how small—run by someone who is not the international marketing manager.

In twenty-five years interviewing firms throughout the world, I have never met a person with the title of international intelligence manager. Do you have one? I am sure you have at least one market researcher who spends some of his or her time going through trade statistics and other published reports. This barely scratches the surface of real market intelligence. Your researchers are probably clerical staff with little or no authority; much of their work may be sporadic, occasional, and not considered a vital function.

Every company in international marketing needs a sustained intelligence effort. You need it even if yours is a small organization with one or two overseas salespeople covering a few priority markets. In fact, the smaller your company, the more concerned you should be with producing intelligence which will help you squeeze all you can out of your limited human resources.

Don't sacrifice intelligence even if your resources are small. An intelligence manager can be a valuable asset. If your budget allows you to put three salespeople in the field and you have not set funds aside for intelligence, get an intelligence manager and sacrifice one of the sales jobs. A good intelligence service will more than make up for it.

If your priority markets include some of the larger countries in Western Europe, you will eventually need a full-time intelligence manager for the area. The same goes for Japan, the United States, and Canada. These are big, attractive, tough, highly competitive markets too important to cover haphazardly and occasionally. If you have not yet succeeded in cracking your biggest and most attractive markets, it could be because of poor or nonexistent intelligence coverage.

A truly international intelligence apparatus, based at your world headquarters, is indispensable. You also need intelligence services at each major branch or regional office around the world.

The Intelligence Manager

Hire your intelligence manager from within your own company. One reason is the morale value of promoting from within. Another is that experienced intelligence managers are rare. You might as well create your own. Do the same at your branch and regional offices. Have an intelligence manager in each one.

Where will your intelligence managers come from? From any department in your company—marketing, administration, finance, statistics, shipping, accounting, personnel. It doesn't matter. What counts is the type of person you choose. Here are some desirable traits.

1. *An inquisitive mind.*   Never satisfied with answers, always asking questions and looking at things from all angles.

2. *Patience.*   It may take months to get a specific bit of intelligence or to find a reliable source.

3. *Persistence.*   A ferret who doesn't give up easily.

4. *Initiative.*   There is no "book" to go by; users of intelligence don't always know what they need.

5. *Imagination.* A valuable trait when looking for sources and trying to learn about a competitor.

6. *An analytical mind.* Intelligence is useless unless converted into action.

7. *A fast and alert reader.* Scanning a report for relevant facts is an art. A person who can do this quickly and is also a voracious reader is uniquely qualified.

8. *Tact.* Indispensable in intelligence when you try to pump people unwilling to talk.

9. *Organization.* Intelligence has to be systematically collated, stored, followed up, and updated.

10. *Self-sufficiency.* Competency in typing, word processing, telexing, communications, computerized filing. (A self-sufficient intelligence manager saves money, promotes the speedy handling of intelligence, and stays fully in the picture at all times.)

Anyone with these qualifications and a knowledge of languages is a rare find. But don't make language ability an indispensable requirement, unless you are a firm in a country where English is not the official language, in which case the intelligence manager must be fluent in English.

Your intelligence service need not be large. A one-person, full-time intelligence manager can easily support an organization of five or six field managers. An assistant can be given the full-time job of developing intelligence from a big market such as West Germany or Japan. In most regional and branch offices, a one-person intelligence service should be enough.

A self-sufficient, computer-literate intelligence manager in a small organization may not need any supporting staff. If your company, on the other hand, is an international giant with subsidiaries or sales offices in twenty countries, agents in eighty others, and a force of fifty traveling representatives and troubleshooters, you need a substantial intelligence department to support them. This could easily mean an intelligence manager, three or four assistants in charge of different areas of the world, a staff of ten or twelve researchers, intelligence reviewers and editors—in addition to intelligence departments run by your branch and regional offices, and subsidiaries.

If you have a market research department, use it as the starting point for a new, vigorous, action-oriented intelligence apparatus.

Intelligence Functions

The five functions of international intelligence are:

1. To define intelligence needs
2. To find sources
3. To collect intelligence
4. To evaluate intelligence
5. To update intelligence

Defining Intelligence Needs

As the intelligence manager, your first task is to decide precisely what intelligence to gather. Turn to your "customers"—salespeople in the field, branch and regional managers, subsidiaries, agents around the world, the international marketing manager, and any other head office executives who need information to plan future moves.

If you are an agent, your intelligence "customers" will also include the manufacturers and suppliers you represent, even though they in turn may evaluate and turn over your information to their field managers and salespeople.

Go over the checklists in Chapter 2 with your intelligence customers, adding or deleting questions. Discuss with the international marketing manager the checklist on the competition, and you will quickly learn how much he or she does not know. Do the same with field salespeople. Soon you will know what intelligence to dig for.

Sift through international files—at your home office and in the field—for useful bits of intelligence which may have been unintentionally buried. This can be a tedious, lengthy, but useful project.

Defining intelligence needs is not a one-time task. Changes in a market or in the competition will create new needs. A shift in government can wipe out VIP contacts. The sudden landing of competitors in a market where you least expected them will raise new requirements for intelligence about agents, prices, promotions, the reliability of sources, the need for new ones. Fluctuations in exchange rates can make markets suddenly more, or less, attractive.

A decision by your company to open a new sales office abroad, or to upgrade a market to priority status, will put new pressures on you to produce new and deeper intelligence.

Local market opportunities also change. If you are an agent you may want to branch out into new fields, which in turn will require a redefinition of your needs for information on suppliers and manufacturers.

Keep in touch with all of your intelligence users, especially field managers and salespeople, by letter, telex, telephone, and as often as possible through personal meetings.

Finding Sources

Seek and evaluate in-house intelligence links, either by canvassing your personnel one by one (possible only in a relatively small organization, or if you confine your search to the main office), or by circulating notices indicating your interest in finding employees with contacts abroad. Send a simple, short questionnaire to all employees, no matter how large your company.

Ask your employees to be specific. You want the names, addresses, jobs, and backgrounds of people they may know abroad. Pick out links with good sources in the countries or cities where your chief competitors are located, in your priority markets, and (if you are an agent) in countries where manufacturers and suppliers of your types of products are located.

Every employee who reads a newspaper from abroad should know that you are interested in anything which might relate to your company and product. Specify the type of information you are looking for, or leave it up to the employee to use his or her judgment. Encourage them to bring you clippings of news items and ads. Again, this request can be made through notices, circular bulletins, or an employee in-house newspaper.

The job of finding intelligence sources is the prime responsibility of the intelligence manager, but everybody has to help, particularly your international sales force. Seek sources actively, not only through in-house links but also by going to the target markets, visiting universities, research institutes, embassy and consular commercial offices.

In the search for sources, the intelligence and marketing managers must learn to work together, compare notes on best contacts, friends and acquaintances around the world. They must decide what intelligence is needed in each market and what are the best types of sources to get it.

The first contact with potential sources can be made by marketing managers, field managers, salespeople, agents, and traveling executives. It is up to the intelligence manager, however, to evaluate sources, meet them in person, cultivate them, and keep them productive. Take regular trips abroad to meet with them, and also to keep your finger on the pulse of each market. These trips have another advantage: they free marketing personnel from intelligence duties and let them concentrate on selling.

Assuming a minimal intelligence operation, how many sources do you need in each priority market abroad? Figure from six to ten. If you select them carefully from the types we discussed in Chapter 4, this will give you good coverage, including two or three candidates for a mini-thinktank. If your company is going after six priority markets, this means keeping track of up to sixty people.

Your rock bottom needs in each country are:

- One source to gather and send you trade reports, statistics, catalogs, newspaper clippings, professional publications
- One source to monitor local pricing, promotion, trade fairs, conventions
- Two sources to develop intelligence on the competition—keeping track of the comings and goings of competitors, their local agents
- Two sources to develop VIP contacts

Don't worry about overlapping. No single source is foolproof and guaranteed. Duplication is a good way to check and double-check intelligence.

In a big, complex, and diversified market, you never have enough sources. To get a good picture of what is happening in West Germany, for instance, you may need to set up and cultivate twenty or more sources.

In countries or cities where your competition is based, the caliber of your sources is vital and there is no way to establish a fixed pattern that works everywhere. You may be lucky to cultivate an inside source, or you may need to hire a discreet consultant. It will take much time and patience, but the target is worth the effort.

If your international operations are so large that you need an elaborate centralized intelligence service, the job of finding and evaluating sources will end up being a full time assignment for at least two or three of your staff, often working in cooperation with your branches, regional offices, and subsidiaries abroad. The number of sources you may need to keep fully informed of what is happening in the front lines will number in the hundreds. You will have to delegate some intelligence authority and responsibility to your offices and subsidiaries abroad. For instance, if you have a well-staffed office in Frankfurt, it should have the main responsibility for "running" all German sources.

Collecting Intelligence

Once you have set up your sources and the flow of intelligence begins to pick up, your first unbending rule must be to insist that all of it be passed on to the main office. Your overseas field managers and salespeople may be tempted to sort out intelligence and send you only what they think is important. Don't let them do it! If you do, you will never get a true picture of what is happening in the field. You will be back to the problem today facing many large international corporations: decisions taken without a clear idea of front-line conditions.

If your subsidiary in Singapore or Stockholm has its own intelligence manager and can use the information locally, so much the better—as long as the item is also relayed to your international headquarters.

An enthusiastic, hard-working intelligence apparatus can easily run into a problem that will gum up the works: overproduction—too much incoming intelligence, not enough time to sort it out. Avoid this problem by going for quality and consigning to the trashcan whatever is not important. Or dump irrelevant information into noncritical files, which is the same as trashing it because the files will soon be bulging with trivia nobody will ever read. Your sales forces will not have time to digest exhaustive reports. Give them three facts they can use rather than twenty five that will put them to sleep.

Stay in touch with your sources, and set up systematic follow-up to remind them of deadlines or the urgency of a particular item. If the information is vital, telephone the source, discuss your requirement and how best to get the information. This can save you days, and will assure you that the source knows exactly what you want. Make the telephone an intelligence tool. Use it often, and instruct your overseas sources to do the same.

Gathering information from associations, embassies, and government agencies must be done systematically. Try to get it by subscription or by phone.

Intelligence from embassy contacts should be collected through personal visits—a job for the intelligence manager or qualified assistants. You don't have to make the rounds of all the embassies, unless your company is ringing doorbells in every corner of the world. In Washington alone there are more than 100 embassies, a full-time job for at least two people! Go after the embassies of the countries you have targeted as priority markets, and the embassies of the countries of your competitors.

A great deal of intelligence will come from the systematic debriefing of company people who have been abroad. Many details and viewpoints will emerge from a debriefing session that would otherwise be quickly forgotten by the traveler.

The same goes for your overseas sources. Try to see them face to face at least once a year and pick their brains. They may have inadvertently left out a lot of useful intelligence from their reports to you.

Evaluation

Evaluation, the crux of market intelligence, is a processing stage between the producer (source) and the user (salesperson or decision-making executive).

Processing long-range, strategic market intelligence involves keeping up with political and economic developments, collating reports, and discussing them frequently with the international marketing manager and other executives.

"Street-level" intelligence seldom requires deep analysis, as in these examples:

> "The Ministry of the Interior may soon be in the market for 1500 rotating beacons for police cars."

> "Local architects are negotiating the design of a new science center for the National University."

This sort of information should be telexed to your nearest salesperson or agent within the hour—"raw."

Some intelligence has to be collated with existing data. For instance:

> "Flavia Bombardini is Italtronic's new field manager in Southeast Asia."

Before you dash off a telex to your salesperson in Singapore, check your files. What do you know about Flavia Bombardini? Is she new, unknown, or was she stationed elsewhere before? Was she involved in any big Italtronic projects? Bring her file up to date (or open one if there is nothing on her), then send your telex.

Intelligence on unexpected activity by a competitor in a market which had been ignored is a sure sign that something is afoot and worth investigating. For instance, a source in Senegal telexes you that the managing director of Xenia Gmbh, your largest German competitor, has just spent five days in Dakar. What's happening in Senegal to warrant such a high-level visit?

Intelligence about the competition—such as latest sales figures, high-level executive appointments, the opening of a new overseas subsidiary or branch, and major contract awards—does not always call for quick action. But it has to be fed into a composite picture, which should at all times reflect the latest intelligence on the competitor. The picture should be brief, concise, clear, and frequently discussed with marketing.

The file should include an evaluation of the competitor's international marketing system, methods, and style, as well as an assessment of the company's marketing executives, field managers and traveling salespeople. Are there any visible common tactics among them? Any evidence of unusual individual initiative?

An agent should keep the same type of files on local competition.

Don't underestimate your competitors. Assume they are strong and effective. The attitude that your product and company are unbeatable and that nobody else knows what they are doing is childish, unbusinesslike, and dangerous.

How far should the intelligence manager evaluate a competitor or market developments? Enough to form an opinion and suggest two or three plans of action. The object of this type of evaluation is to stimulate discussion and an eventual decision based on the best available intelligence. It is easier to discuss an issue when a motion has been put forward. The intelligence manager must submit motions, even though they may be rejected.

As the intelligence manager you must resist self-censorship—hiding or throwing out information which clashes with the views of other executives. And don't water down your reports with too many qualifiers in order to cover yourself. Neither situation is healthy. They weaken intelligence. Drill this lesson into all branch and regional managers. Insist that they send you factual, unadulterated reports.

Processing intelligence is essentially subjective. The intelligence manager must form opinions. He or she also must decide what intelligence to discard. For some people this is a problem. The natural reaction of a bureaucrat is to file everything—the quickest way to kill an intelligence operation. This process of subjective evaluation and selection should be done only at the main office, by the international intelligence manager or close assistants.

At the branch and regional level, managers should be free to go through incoming intelligence to pick out information of immediate use, and should be encouraged to pass on their own evaluations, along with *all* raw, incoming data and reports.

A lot of intelligence picked up at debriefings of company employees is useless. Get rid of it quickly, but don't discourage the employees who brought it.

Make your reports to the international marketing manager, other executives, and field personnel short and direct. If the information is important, telex or phone it. Don't let any information sit on your desk more than twenty-four hours. Don't be too concerned with form and style.

Updating Intelligence

To stay *live*, intelligence has to be filed and frequently updated. The best way to do this is with a personal computer. Create an intelligence databank on countries, competitors, and individuals (executives, salespeople, end users, VIPs).

The files should be flexible and easy to access, edit, and merge. In short, use a word processing program. (Databank management software is too rigid—data categories have to be carefully defined by headings and fields, forcing you to adapt the intelligence item to the format, and you risk losing important information because you may not know exactly where to enter it.)

Start with a few basic files. Keep the menu short. Resist the tendency to set up dozens of files by title before you have anything to put into them. All you will accomplish is to clutter up your intelligence bank needlessly.

The more files you have, the easier it is to forget where you put something.

Eventually some subdividing of files is inevitable, especially files that go beyond ten or twelve pages. Minimize this by editing each time you make a new entry in a file. This is no major problem if you are not afraid to use a knife. Street-level intelligence can quickly go stale.

Delete and condense as much as you can. Whenever you have made a change in a file, run a printout. Or do a printout every two or three weeks. *You will see things on paper that escaped you on your monitor's screen.*

In addition to presenting the condensed current intelligence on a competitor, a country, or an individual, each file should also have your latest assessment on how it affects your company's position and what action you suggest.

Your intelligence databank can be a live marketing tool if you remember these three basic rules:

1. Don't clutter.
2. Make it brief.
3. Keep editing.

Delivering Intelligence

Long-range, strategic intelligence does not call for immediate delivery. Information on market and business developments in South Korea, for instance, can be condensed into a comprehensive report to be discussed eventually with the international marketing manager and the salesperson responsible for Asia. If South Korea is already a priority market, this type of review should occur regularly—at least once a month.

If South Korea is not a priority market, but you think it should be, submit a report with a specific plan of action, perhaps even suggesting possible local agents. Be short and to the point.

Street-level intelligence should be delivered directly to the people who can act on it right away: the international marketing manager, field managers, salespeople, or agents. The shorter the line between the intelligence manager and the user of the intelligence, the less chances the information will go stale or become distorted, the more value a front-line salesperson will get out of it.

International marketing managers are the top "customers" of company intelligence services. They often insist on getting raw intelligence which they will then evaluate and hopefully do something about. A word of caution: Don't expect them to use all the information you deliver to them. After all, the final decision is theirs. International marketing is their responsibility.

A smooth-flowing intelligence service, therefore, depends not only on the ability of the intelligence manager but also on the enthusiastic support of the marketing people. One of the main functions of the intelligence manager is to develop close rapport with marketing—the best guarantee that intelligence will be used at the tactical level.

There is no need to hide the intelligence databank behind a curtain of secret passwords and procedures. The deeper you bury intelligence, the less you will use it. A lot can be said for confidentiality, but the ultimate reason for intelligence is to help you improve your sales. Unless the intelligence is readily available to your users, you will have wasted it. If you have computer links to your regional and branch offices around the world, you will have an ideal way to keep everybody instantly updated on file changes.

The Cost of an Intelligence Service

A minimal, one-person, full-time intelligence service will cost you from $70,000 to $75,000 a year. This budget will work for a small or for a large company and includes the following:

A. Intelligence manager	$ 30,000
B. Travel by the intelligence manager	20,000
C. Telephone, telex, postage, couriers	6,000
D. Sources in priority markets	15,000
E. Subscriptions	1,000
Total	$ 72,000

Your *real* cost is lower. Let us say that you have promoted someone who had a $24,000 salary, and you find that the person's previous functions can be taken over by others in the company *without* hiring new talent from the outside. Your additional salary expense is only $6,000.

You may already be subscribing to half of the publications you need. Your real new budget for subscriptions becomes $500.

Your total real budget is reduced to $47,500.

Travel and communications should *not* be slashed. The estimated

$20,000 allows the intelligence manager to be abroad for twelve to fifteen weeks a year, including airline fares and all other expenses.

The more the intelligence manager travels abroad, the less need for salespeople to spend time getting intelligence. *Their* travel can be shortened (saving you money), or kept the same (more time to sell). Another bonus: Any intelligence you gather abroad about your competition—product development, personnel changes, marketing tactics—will be useful to *domestic* marketing. Don't forget that *your domestic market is somebody else's export market.*

You can get a lot of mileage out of a *real* investment of less than $50,000, with benefits to your international *and* domestic marketing departments.

If you assign a full-time intelligence manager to a big market such as some of the Western European countries, you will have to add at least 50 percent to your budget. This could easily double if you are operating in several countries or regions and have to support a sales force of half a dozen field managers and salespeople.

The Value of Consultants

International marketing consultants can be productive, *if you let them.* Don't retain one unless you have a specific assignment in mind. When clients are not specific, they are (1) ignorant and don't really know what they are looking for, (2) too lazy to take the time and effort to lay down objectives, or (3) they expect a consultant to go on a fishing expedition to see what comes up.

If you are ignorant, do your homework *before* you talk to a consultant. Being lazy is no excuse. Going fishing is silly even if you have money to burn.

When you hire a consultant, *you* should be in the driver's seat. Narrow down your questions. Develop as much information as you can on your own. A lot of the real work will be done in the target country by street-level sources. The difference is that the cost of these sources is a fraction of what a consultant may charge you by the time the information is expanded and embellished into long dissertations, complete with charts, slides, and forecasts.

A teaching aids manufacturer once asked me to do a market feasibility study of an Asian market. With the help of a local assistant, I gathered the information and delivered a twenty-page report in six weeks.

Meanwhile, back at my client's conglomerate headquarters, someone had hired a high-powered international consulting firm to do the same job (without telling the people I was dealing with). Five months later the firm submitted an impressive report of more than 200 pages, delivered by a "team" from the consulting firm who insisted on making a two-hour presentation.

The conclusions were the same as mine. The cost, I was told confidentially, came to more than ten times my fee.

I am not trying to pooh-pooh consultants. After all, I have been making my living as one. I am suggesting, however, that you use them wisely and economically. Point them in the right direction and they will pay off.

Intelligence and Sales Power

A tight, well-run intelligence service can give your sales force extra power and weapons against the competition, but intelligence is not an end in itself, only a tool. No matter how well connected your sources, how smart your thinktanks, how thorough your intelligence databank, how receptive your executives, the moment of truth comes when somewhere in one of your markets abroad one of your salespeople meets a buyer. Everything hinges on the outcome of this encounter.

Let's look at manpower and how to get the most out of it.

PART 2

Boosting Your Striking Power

6

A Mobile, Hard-Hitting Sales Force

How many saleswomen and salesmen can you put in the field? Where will they come from? How quickly can you deploy them? How will you use them? What will make them better than your competitors' sales forces?

No matter what happens at headquarters, the performance of your action zone troops decides how well you do in your international markets. Their striking power depends on:

- Numbers
- Mobility
- Concentration
- Quality
- Global teamwork

The Size of Your Sales Force

One way to figure out how many salespeople you need is to create territories and dole them out one territory to one salesperson. The other is to send out as many people as you can afford to sustain in overseas travel, *regardless of the number of territories*, and to use them where they can do you the most good.

Try the second approach. It is flexible. It lets you use your sales power creatively. It pays off.

Your limiting factor is budget. If your salespeople travel a third of their time (about right in most situations), you are probably spending about $20,000 a year each on travel. How much each additional investment of $20,000 can bring you in added sales only you can tell, in terms of your product and end users. Salary and benefits need not be a major additional cost if you recruit from within the company.

How many salespeople is enough? Aside from budget, one guideline is to estimate potential sales in your priority overseas markets. If budget is not a serious problem, sales potential seems high, and you hold a favorable competitive edge, send in as many people as you can.

Earlier I mentioned a firm which hired exactly one field manager for each of five overseas territories established arbitrarily. This is not unlike the case of the Texas town which called the Texas Rangers to help put down a local riot. When a solitary ranger got off the train, a puzzled mayor asked, "Just one of you?" The ranger replied: "There's only one riot, isn't there?"

Marketing, of course, is not a question of putting out fires but of aggressively going after sales, wherever you can get them. A friend of mine recently appointed export manager for a German manufacturer of electrical machinery approached his assignment a bit differently.

"Give me all the men and women in the company who have selling experience and let me put them on the line," he asked his managing director. He didn't get his wish entirely, but he did manage to pick up three additional people whose talents had been wasted in departments which had nothing to do with marketing.

Add numbers to your sales force by recruiting and training new blood from within the company. Don't go outside unless absolutely necessary. Every company has hidden sales talent. This waste occurs particularly in companies overloaded with nonproductive support staff because not everybody is eager to take on a selling assignment. Selling is a pressure job. Most managers make it so. They pit people against one another like gladiators, not realizing that some individuals react negatively to this sort of treatment yet could be productive if left to handle situations on their own.

Comb through your personnel files for new sales recruits. If you or a recruit are not sure if a job in sales will work out, assign him or her to international marketing on a trial basis, keeping the old job open in case the arrangement does not work out. Use the estimated $20,000 travel budget, or your own figures, as a rule of thumb to decide how many people you can afford to put in the field.

Numbers are not everything, but the more people you have in the field, regular or irregular, the more you should sell. Put as many active salespeople "on the line" as you can afford. In the next chapter we will look at the use of "irregular" forces and how they can enhance your striking power. Develop a plan to work with irregulars and you may easily double or triple your *real* striking power at minimal cost.

Another way of doing it is through a new weapon in creative international marketing—the rapid-deployment sales force.

Mobility, Concentration— and Your Own RDF

In creative international marketing, mobility and concentration involve the ability to respond quickly to business opportunities and the application of sales power where it can be most effective. For this you need a well-trained, flexible sales force ready to be used anywhere in the world: a rapid-deployment force (RDF). It can be one of the deadliest new weapons in your arsenal.

Why an RDF? If yours is a small international operation, you may have two or three regional managers assigned to specific territories. If yours is a massive international organization, you probably have branches, regional offices, and subsidiaries firmly established in many cities. In both cases you are tying down sales personnel. There is more flexibility in a smaller firm, but regional managers still have their rounds to make, several countries to cover; they seldom are able to stay long enough to follow up. A large firm with established branches cannot afford to have a floating sales crew, here today, gone tomorrow, to go after its biggest markets. The fact that a branch or regional office, or a subsidiary, has been established is proof that the market deserves priority.

In both cases you can benefit enormously from having additional power—a rapid-deployment force not frozen to a specific territory or office.

The concept of mobility and concentration clashes with the conventional idea of fixed territories. One territory, one salesperson sounds neat, but in the long run it may cost you sales, unless you also have an RDF. *The idea of fixed territories implies a dispersal of sales forces.* This problem is compounded when some of your sales forces are not fully occupied, as in the following typical situation.

Business is booming in Indonesia, Singapore, Malaysia, Thailand, and Hong Kong. Your field manager in Singapore can barely manage to get home for a change of clothes before dashing off on another trip. There is no time to keep up with all leads, to make all the presentations, to reach all prospects, *and to follow up.*

Meanwhile, your field manager in Africa is finding the going slow, has little to do, spends most of her time keeping in touch with potential end users and government officials.

If yours is a traditional, conservative firm, you will tell your Southeast Asia manager to "Cope as best you can!"; you will be happy with the flow of sales and never give a thought to all the additional business you could be getting if you had more manpower in the area. You advise the one in Africa to "Keep trying!" You will be neglecting valuable sales opportunities in one territory while wasting a competent salesperson in another.

If you are a tactics-oriented international marketing manager you will quickly put Africa on a back burner and shift its field manager to Singapore to lend a hand. If necessary you will pull people from other lukewarm territories. In fact, if business in Southeast Asia is truly sizzling, you should even seek sales reinforcements from your domestic division!

Most of the time a regional manager spends making the rounds of a territory is wasted on travel. On a three-week trip, the actual time spent face to face with prospective buyers—real selling time—can probably be measured in *hours*.

Tight travel schedules allow little flexibility. There is always a plane to catch tomorrow or the day after. The busy field manager invariably leaves it up to a local agent to follow up and keeps his or her fingers crossed that the job won't be botched up because the moment you turn a deal over to an agent your chances of success will shrink. The agent has other fish to fry, or will not be able to answer all of the questions the buyer will raise without telexing your home office.

Here are two facts of international marketing worth memorizing:

1. Nobody can sell your product better than your own salespeople.

2. Many international sales are lost to poor follow-up.

Even if yours is a large international concern, you cannot possibly have a salesperson sitting on every pending deal around the world. Which is why wasting sales talent is inexcusable. For Nancy Niles to twiddle her thumbs in Latin America, where sales prospects for her company's product are slim, is like looking for a job in Saudi Arabia for a Norwegian ski instructor. Besides, idle manpower is bad for morale. Good salespeople need to sell, to be turned loose on favorable hunting grounds.

If you have five salespeople and two are in stagnant territories, you are wasting 40 percent of your striking power. Measure your waste by what the two idle salespeople could produce if allowed to operate in a *live* market.

If all five salespeople are going full tilt and still cannot cope with all the business coming at them, pour more forces into the fray. Don't lose momentum!

For some European manufacturers of science products, the tactics of mobility and concentration are working well in Algeria, where business is booming and there are no local firms to represent foreign manufacturers and suppliers (the answer is to have your own sales office). One manufacturer has a full-time team in Algeria of six salespeople selling directly to schools, universities, polytechnics, research, and health institutions—a much bigger and more concentrated attack than the firm has launched in the rest of Africa and the Middle East combined.

West German science manufacturers are also concentrating sales power in Spain and Turkey. French firms are systematically going after the French-speaking countries of Africa.

Let's go back to our hypothetical situation in Southeast Asia. Suppose that even though things are sizzling there, you can't send in reinforcements from other territories because everybody is busy. The answer is your RDF. Send in one, two, or three people—whatever immediate reinforcements are needed.

The RDF can be made up of one person or fifty, depending on the size of your company. Who is assigned to an RDF? New sales talent, preferably from within the company—people thoroughly trained on product and company, who can be expected to put on a creditable presentation. They should be young, unattached, ready to travel wherever and whenever needed.

To be fully mobile and effective, the RDF must be under your international marketing office. This does not imply that its members must sit around playing cards in a "ready room" waiting for a call for action. If your budget allows, keep members of your RDF busy on overseas assignments at all times—whether on short visits to help a local salesperson or agent, or on longer, unspecified stays. Scatter them around the world wherever they can be useful. Use them in response to leads from less important countries not normally covered by your sales force. Shift them from time to time; the more exposure they get to different market conditions, the better their training and long-range usefulness to the company. Don't let them linger in a country unless there is still a job to be done.

To make the RDF work effectively, you must impress upon everybody in your organization that RDF overseas assignments are not permanent.

If you cannot afford to keep your entire RDF out in the field all the time, assign some of them to in-house support jobs at the main office. To keep everybody sharp, rotate them so that all have a taste of overseas action from time to time.

Eventually RDF members will graduate to more permanent assignments abroad—as branch or regional managers, for instance. Low-priority markets may suddenly come alive, or you may need permanent reinforcements in another territory. Recruiting and training an RDF, therefore, must be a never-ending process.

Mobility and concentration in the use of international sales power call for imagination, flexible thinking, speedy action, and *guts*. The concept flies in the face of conventional marketing methods. Try it—combine your permanent sales force with the flexibility of a well-trained RDF—and you soon will be running circles around your competition. This is not for the complacent international marketing manager who likes to run a smooth-sailing ship. Mobility and concentration require careful monitoring of conditions in priority markets, and being wide awake to openings elsewhere. This is where you get your money's worth from an effective intelligence service.

A good example of the use of mobility and concentration is the invasion of the Chinese market by more than 300 Japanese firms, most of them employing dozens of salespeople and technicians reaching into every corner of the country. In contrast, most European and U.S. firms cover China through occasional visits by lone travelers, who seldom spend more than a few days in Beijing and Shanghai.

Japanese firms are next door to China. European firms concentrating on Turkey, Algeria, and other African markets are also capitalizing on proximity—being able to deploy salespeople quickly in response to calls for presentations, quotations, and follow-up. However, mobility and concentration have also worked well for U.S. and Japanese firms in distant markets like Saudi Arabia. Logistics becomes more complicated, travel costlier, but the ultimate determining factor is opportunity, not distance.

The secret is to strike where the opposition is softest and opportunities best. Concentrate your forces, whether yours is a small company with limited personnel, or a large operation with an army of salespeople in the field. Combine the strength of your permanent salespeople in the field, with the added muscle of a nimble RDF.

A word of warning: Be careful how you shift sales forces in or out of big markets—Europe, Japan, the United States, Canada. *Pour in* all the sales power at your command once you have cracked any of them, but be reluctant to take sales forces *away* from them unless the situation is hopeless. These are markets which don't go up and down roller-coaster fashion. If you stand a chance to succeed in any of them, it will be through a combination of strong sales power (including ready reserves), promotion, thorough intelligence, persistence, and patience. You either go into these markets with all you've got, or you stay away. *To achieve success in any of them is worth taking forces away from other parts of the world.* If any of the big markets is on your priority list, make sure that *everybody* in your RDF is trained accordingly.

How much sales power to use and where to concentrate it also depends on how effective your local agents are. Smart agents who work hand in glove with their suppliers can absorb a lot of the sales pressure if they know how to keep their own salespeople on their toes—well trained, well motivated, well paid, and, above all, capable of systematic and professional follow up. This is a major asset to any international supplier.

On the other hand, agents who lose interest the moment the supplier's field manager or salesperson walks out the door are cutting their own throats in the long run. If the business outlook is good but the agent is lackadaisical, sooner or later the supplier will either send in more salespeople or start scouting around for another agent.

The Quality of Your Sales Force

Superstar performers are rare. You may or may not have some in your sales force. In all likelihood your salespeople start off no better or worse equipped to go after overseas markets than your competitors'. People with exceptional talents are as rare in international marketing as in any other line of work.

You can, however, sharpen your sales force—including your RDF—and give it a *quality* edge over your competitors. Quality makes the difference. It depends on many things. Here are some of them.

1. *Know your product, know your company.* A basic, logical principle not always followed. You would be surprised how often one runs into salespeople halfway around the world who are able to do little more than thumb through brochures. I have yet to see a brochure that answered all my questions. If I am a buyer in Kano, Nigeria, and you, the salesperson, cannot tell me what I want to know about your product, not even give me a price, I am likely to bid you goodbye and turn to the nearest competitor before your plane back to Lagos is off the ground.

The farther away salespeople are from their home office, the more thoroughly they must know their product and company.

2. *Training.* Beyond product and company knowledge, how realistic and intensive is your training? How do you prepare your salespeople to face conditions in the field?

You may be wasting too much time sending people to sales seminars created for domestic markets that have little bearing on international selling. Nothing is more boring to an international salesperson than to sit through two or three days of ecstatic presentations on how to handle objections and how to close a sale, when deals back in his or her territory are perhaps decided by "Who do you know?" and "What's in it for me?" or by government bid committees you never meet in person.

3. *Morale.* The perennial gripe among international salespeople is that they are seldom understood by the home office. They often feel let down, lonely, out on a limb. Remember Dianne Baker, back in Chapter 1, and how her boss shot down her wind-powered generator project in Turkey?

Morale is also weakened when a company sets up rigid sales quotas and bonuses regardless of conditions in the field. Here's a typical case:

Jim Arnold, Middle East field manager for World Trading Services, has a very good year, goes over his quota, and earns a $5000 bonus. Halfway around the world, Nancy Niles, responsible for Latin America, falls short of her sales target. She does not get a bonus.

Jim's territory is affluent, he has a lot of agents, business is booming, there are no local industry or import controls in most of the countries he covers. Nancy has a problem. Brazil has its own industry; import licenses are hard to get. Argentina, Peru, and Venezuela are up to their ears in international debts. She has four big orders hanging fire, but for lack of foreign exchange they are postponed and included in next year's budget. These situations are entirely beyond her control. She gets penalized just the same.

Can you blame Nancy if she begins to entertain unprintable thoughts about her company and decides to investigate job opportunities with more understanding competitors?

Treat salespeople fairly, give them your full support, make them feel you are behind them all the way, build up their enthusiasm. A salesperson in a negative frame of mind will cost you sales. A positive frame of mind spells quality.

4. *Information.*   We have already looked in detail at intelligence. You never know enough, and this goes for salespeople as well. Never assume they have all the facts about local markets and competitors. Feed them the latest intelligence summary on the country or agent about to be visited. The quality of a salesperson's performance depends a lot on being thoroughly briefed before setting out on a selling trip.

5. *Education and background.*   Although most of the people in international marketing are not linguists, salespeople who speak one or more foreign languages are major assets. A knowledge of history, culture, religions, and politics also gives quality to your sales force. Keep this in mind when you search your employee records for new international marketing recruits. Your Lebanese assistant cashier may be more useful to you as a salesperson covering the Middle East than counting money back home.

6. *Tact and manners.*   How a salesperson acts, talks, eats, dresses, and behaves is vital in face-to-face encounters with agents, VIPs, and potential end users. Tactful, low-key salespeople are rare. They still command the respect and attention of people around the world. If you have any, you may have a definite advantage over your competition.

7. *Job stability.*   When you work as an international salesperson, you may well wonder if while you are beating the bushes in Peru someone back home is gunning for your job or beating you to a promotion. This is a legitimate concern. Another is, what happens if you don't meet your quota, as in the case of Nancy Niles? Will headquarters understand the situation (assuming it is out of your control), or does your neck go on the chopping block?

One thing you don't need in international marketing is worried salespeople. Japanese companies notoriously are good at making people feel secure in their jobs. At the other extreme are companies in the United

States where executives seem to be perennially engaged in a game of musical chairs.

In international marketing the secret is to select your salespeople with care and to give them your support and confidence when you are convinced they have the right qualifications. Don't rush to send people into the field. And remember, if you switch an employee to international marketing on a trial basis, keep his or her old job open, just in case.

The quality of your international sales force will go up several notches if your salespeople don't have to keep looking over their shoulders.

8. *Motivation and career goals.* What motivates an international marketing person? Money and promotion are obvious answers, as in most jobs. A third is a desire to "see the world," but this can wear thin quickly.

If an international salesperson is interested in money and promotion, sooner or later you, the employer, will have to pull him or her out of international marketing and into another department in the company. Aside from the constant risk of promoting someone to his or her level of incompetence, you lose an experienced salesperson. You can't help it. If future promotions are not in the cards, the salesperson may eventually quit, anyhow. An executive ladder climber will not want to travel internationally forever and stay out of touch with internal company politics.

Some international salespeople are motivated strictly by money. Promotion is not important, as long as they earn a good living and get reasonable salary increases or bonuses from time to time. They enjoy travel and may even get itchy if they have to stay home for too long. These people are easier to deal with than promotion-oriented salespeople.

A clear understanding of precisely what international salespeople expect from their jobs, and your assurance that they stand every chance of achieving their goals, are vital to developing a quality international sales force.

9. *Reasonable travel.* A tired sales force quickly loses its punch. Don't drive salespeople to exhaustion by keeping them on the road for weeks on end. International travel is hectic. In addition to the normal aggravations—long hours in airport lounges, delayed flights, bad food, impersonal hotel rooms, poor service—the international traveler has to put up with jetlag, customs and immigrations checks, money exchange, changing habits, cultures, and languages.

Everybody has an endurance threshhold beyond which performance begins to sag. Mine is three or four weeks. Other international salespeople can stay out longer. Some are ready to come home after two weeks.

Discuss this problem with each salesperson. If someone can perform for four or five weeks and is happy with this schedule, take advantage of it. If another one, for whatever reason, cannot or will not take the pressure for more than three weeks, make adjustments.

Reasonable travel means different things to different salespeople. Don't apply the same formula to everybody.

10. *Accompanied travel.*   Add a touch of class to your international sales force by occasionally allowing your salespeople to travel with their spouses. The investment is minimal, your potential gains high. You help your salespeople develop better social ties with agents, customers, and VIPs. You boost the morale of your sales forces. You encourage agents and VIPs to loosen up, perhaps drop valuable bits of intelligence. You can keep salespeople on the road longer.

Two of the most successful and effective international salespeople I have met in twenty-five years of travel, both employed by a U.S. electronics manufacturer, invariably take their wives with them on all trips at company expense. They have developed and maintained one of the most effective and loyal marketing networks based on strong business and personal ties with agents all over the world.

Traveling with a spouse is unusual, except at high executive levels. Companies who allow it at the "working level" have learned that it can pay off.

Clear Objectives

Apply your striking power where it can generate sales and profits. Don't waste salespeople where someone else in your company can do a better job. In many international marketing situations a better job can be done by people whose prime talents are *not* selling.

Let's look again at the case of Nancy Niles—unable to produce orders in her territory for reasons beyond her control. You are wasting Nancy's valuable sales talent, but you don't want to abandon the territory entirely. What do you do?

Simple. Send Nancy where business is booming, and assign someone else to keep an eye on her dormant territory. Who? If you merely want to keep in touch with VIPs, end users, and potential agents, send a *diplomat*— someone good at shaking hands, taking people to lunch, and kissing babies. All you want to do is keep up the goodwill. This public relations exercise can be handled by any number of company executives, and it does not require intensive travel and expense.

If your goal is licensing or joint-venture manufacturing, send a *negotiator* or an *engineer*, depending on which stage of the negotiations you happen to be at and what questions have to be answered.

If a market is temporarily dead but you have a loyal, local agent who will stick by you hoping for better times ahead, make sure someone drops by for a visit from time to time to keep the ties solid. Don't ignore agents simply because market conditions have put a lid on their sales efforts. Tomorrow you may be happy they stuck to you.

In these situations an infusion of salesmanship will help—as in any business dealing—but is not critical. Your salespeople—including your RDF—are your elite strike force. Save them for straight selling situations.

Deciding what type of personnel to send on a particular mission implies having a clear idea of your objectives. What do you want to achieve in a country or territory? Is it urgent? What level of manpower will you need?

Many overseas public relations, goodwill assignments can be carried out by junior personnel or staff, even by employees on holidays abroad, depending on how important the mission is.

Using diplomats, negotiators, engineers, financial people, and others not involved directly in marketing boosts your striking power by freeing your sales force from nonselling assignments and by exposing more of your people to the international marketplace.

Clear objectives can help you reduce manpower waste in other ways. Sending out too many salespeople on a selling assignment is as bad as not sending enough, to say nothing of additional travel costs. The same goes for sending out teams of salespeople and technicians on trips. This is impressive and often desirable, but if the salesperson is well trained and the presentations are not expected to go into deep technical detail, sending a technician can be a waste.

International marketing objectives have to be realistic. Don't set yourself impossible tasks—such as reaching sales figures that require a field force twice as big as you have or can afford to send out.

Make a list of your overseas targets, decide what personnel you need to achieve them, and figure out who is best qualified for each job. For targets which clearly call for salespeople, you also have to decide when and how far to use your RDF and what you expect them to accomplish. Do the same on a local basis if you are an agent.

Global Teamwork

The territorial concept and its implied dispersal of sales forces does not always promote teamwork. Salespeople are frozen into fixed compartments, get together only occasionally at international meetings or trade fairs, know little about what is happening outside their bailiwicks, and are often made to compete against each other.

In short, they don't think global!

The effective use of personnel in international marketing depends on teamwork. Encourage everybody to think global. You may have assigned a field manager to Latin America, one to the Middle East, and a third one to the Far East. Each one is going after a defined priority market. No problem, as long as you encourage all three of them to take an interest in what is going on elsewhere.

You can do this partially through training. You can also ask field managers to suggest ideas on how to improve sales in other territories, without creating internal jealousies and suspicions.

Make your field managers and salespeople part of an informal advisory group which you can tap frequently for constructive and productive advice.

Try not to station salespeople abroad. Keeping your international salespeople back home will encourage them to work together and understand each other's problems. You will promote teamwork and save a lot of money.

The moment a salesperson sets up shop overseas, you have sacrificed mobility, especially if the person has a family. Finding living quarters, shipping furniture and household effects, arranging schooling for children, buying a car, hiring help, getting residents' permits and drivers' licenses can waste months of a salesperson's time.

The cost of shifting someone to an overseas location can be staggering. If the territory does not pan out, you cannot cut your losses and run overnight, and you may find yourself out on a limb, as happened not long ago to a European manufacturer of personal computers.

A regional manager was sent to Hong Kong to develop sales throughout Southeast Asia and China—a dubious assignment because intelligence should have pointed out that low-cost compatibles made in Taiwan, South Korea, and China have made this a tough market, and that in actual potential individual computer buyers the market amounts to a fraction of the European market. Six months of intensive travel in the area brought the message home with a bang.

Meanwhile, the regional manager in West Germany was up to her neck building a dealer network. For the international marketing manager, whose concern was to produce sales and profits as quickly as possible, the decision was clear: Pull out of Southeast Asia, send more people to West Germany.

The regional manager in Southeast Asia, now at last settled in Hong Kong, was transferred to West Germany. Once again he had to go through the exasperating business of shifting his household. For three months the manufacturer had to put up with the unusual and costly situation of a salesperson covering West Germany out of the company's head office in a neighboring country, and occasionally going "home to Hong Kong" for a short visit with his family.

Stationing your own salespeople abroad is an excellent idea when you have cracked a major market—definitely when it happens to be one of the big ones such as the United Kingdom, West Germany, France, or Japan. In these markets you would be foolish to shift people around every few months. You can still promote global thinking even among salespeople assigned more or less permanently to overseas posts. Keep them "in the picture" through reports, frequent meetings, visits.

How you pay your international salespeople also has much to do with global teamwork and esprit de corps. The first instinct of management in most companies is to put salespeople on a commission basis. One reason is incentive, the other is to save money if the person does not produce. In international marketing this can alienate your sales force and create internal rivalries that may deflate your striking power more effectively than your most pugnacious competitor.

If a market is not right for your product, the incentive of a big commission, a new Rolls-Royce every five years, and free vacations in a tropical paradise will not help a field manager boost his or her sales.

You may save money today, but you will have lost tomorrow's sales and profits. Sooner or later a disgruntled salesperson will seek greener meadows.

You don't have to pay everybody the same salary; seniority and experience have to be figured into your payment scheme. Recruits and reserve salespeople in your RDF obviously should not be paid on the same scale as a veteran of many years' standing. Establishing an incentive beyond salary is a good idea if you make it equitable. For instance, set a global sales goal and announce a bonus to be shared by all the salespeople in the field. This is not a foolproof system. Someone will always swear that everybody else got a bonus thanks to his or her efforts. But in the long run it will promote teamwork and minimize jealousies.

Develop teamwork, use your sales force intelligently, put as many people on the line as you can, create a swift RDF, and establish clear objectives. You will have a regular sales force with a striking power far beyond its actual numbers. Complement it with a force of "irregulars," and you will be hard to beat.

7

The Nakodo Factor

On a business trip to an Arabian Gulf country, Larry Dorsett, an independent traveling representative for several European and U.S. companies, was introduced to the Deputy Minister of the Interior by a mutual friend.

"I need facsimile machines," the deputy said.

"That's a bit out of my line," Larry said. "I sell wall-to-wall carpeting."

"Can't you make me an offer?" the deputy insisted. "I must have catalogs and prices as soon as possible."

A smart, alert international salesman, Larry followed his basic rule of business: *Look into every deal, never say no.*

Back in his hotel he pulled out his black book and started looking up addresses. His friend Michel in Geneva should be able to help. He phoned Michel and told him what he was looking for. Three days later, on his way back from the Gulf, Larry stopped in Geneva. Michel had already contacted a German manufacturer interested in the deal. Together they visited the factory, collected and sent catalogs and specifications to the deputy, along with a proposal.

Things didn't happen overnight. Nobody expected them to. But eventually the deal went through, the equipment was delivered and installed, the manufacturer happily and promptly paid Larry and Michel their commission and encouraged them to look for more projects.

There is nothing unique about this sort of business. It happens every day, wherever people are buying and selling. The international sales of many manufacturers and suppliers would dwindle to a trickle if it were not for people like Larry and Michel. The sales of many other companies could go up substantially if only their management were not obtuse and provincial about working with independents.

Call them bird dogs, five percenters, consultants, middlemen—they are invariably active, alert, profit-oriented, independent individuals who can sniff a deal and help make it come about. I call this type of person a *nakodo* (nah-KOH-do)—the Japanese word for a go-between or matchmaker—an independent individual alert to opportunities to earn a buck.

Encourage nakodos and you will acquire an irregular sales force which in some parts of the world can be as effective as your own salespeople and agents. Nakodos sink or swim on their own. They have no corporate structure to prop them up. They may in some cases take a much more serious interest in seeing a deal go through than your own salaried people.

Firms which discourage nakodos are narrow-minded. Statements such as "It is our policy not to work with outsiders," are pompous. All they accomplish is to make nakodos turn to more receptive firms.

Being a nakodo is a legitimate occupation, and should not be associated with under-the-table dealings. Over the years I have personally met dozens of nakodos all over the world. Most of them like to work with Japanese, West German, Swiss, and Scandinavian companies, but too many of them are given the cold shoulder by U.S. firms. They have no end of troubles collecting their commissions, even after manufacturers have been paid in full and the deals concluded and closed. Not that these problems don't happen with European and Japanese firms. But as a rule, nakodos feel that U.S. firms don't understand the nakodo system, and that they, therefore, cannot be trusted.

Actually, some of the biggest all time nakodo deals have involved large U.S. corporations, invariably negotiated at the highest corporate levels, with commissions often running into the tens of millions of dollars.

Companies reluctant to do business with nakodos fear that in most cases nakodo commissions are bribes that are passed on to government officials. They remember the Lockheed scandals in the Middle East in the 1970s. Throughout the world, however, nakodo commissions are seen as legitimate fees for services rendered.

Big-time nakodo deals will go on. However, they are always negotiated in secret and not ostensibly as part of company policy. To protect themselves, lower-echelon marketing executives in many U.S. and European firms prefer to view an outsider with a jaundiced eye. Why take chances? Their suspicion of nakodos often leads them to turn over nakodo inquiries to their legal departments, which in many cases is like kissing the deal goodbye. By the time a cautious lawyer figures out what sort of contract to submit to a nakodo, the deal has gone stale or the nakodo has gone looking for a quicker competitor.

If your official policy is to pay no commissions to outsiders other than "authorized representatives," you are automatically cutting yourself off from a lot of business. You should take a serious look at your policy and figure out if it makes sense. Chances are that if a high-power nakodo approaches your chief executive officer with a $200 million deal, he or she will not be shown to the door. So why not encourage nakodos also at the day-to-day level? Are you afraid that a nakodo may be fronting for a decision-making government official? A purchasing agent in the end user's office? Perhaps a corrupt prince or president? The risk of this being the case is higher on big multimillion-dollar deals than on daily bread-and-butter business.

In the United States, the law prohibits companies from making payments to foreign officials or politicians to help you get government business. This prohibition extends to agents, *if the U.S. company knows or has reason to know that bribing an official is the agent's intention*. You can get around this by not asking any questions. Small payments to minor officials to speed up routine duties—such as license applications or customs clearances—are not included in the U.S. prohibition.

At the local level, agents in many countries are well aware of the value of nakodos in the right places, and will make full use of them whenever and wherever they can.

Why Use Nakodos?

A nakodo force is a cheap way to increase your international sales. There are many reasons why you should use nakodos to boost your international sales.

1. *A bigger sales force.*   Success in marketing has a lot to do with the size of your sales force. You never have enough salespeople, your RDF will never be large enough. Each individual, no matter how talented and exceptional, can deal with only one customer at a time.

As we saw in the preceding chapter, the size of your strike force is limited by how many talented salespeople you have in your company, and how many of them you can afford to put on the front line.

2. *Nakodos cost you nothing.*   They are paid for results. You don't have to underwrite any of their expenses, and you don't even have a cash flow problem because nakodos get paid after you receive your money.

3. *Mystify the competition.*   Encourage nakodos, and your competition will not know where you will strike next. You can easily pinpoint salespeople, field managers, agents, and the priority markets you are hitting hardest. You cannot shadow a force of irregulars.

4. *Collect intelligence.*   Nakodos can bring you valuable information from the field. But remember that their main concern is to sell and earn commissions. Don't expect much information from them.

5. *Boost sales in your priority markets.*   If intelligence shows that Turkey is booming and you don't have enough people to cover it, nakodos can help ferret out business in provinces or among end users overlooked by your salespeople.

6. *Get business in nonpriority markets.* Just because your focus is on six or seven top countries, you don't want to ignore business elsewhere. Nakodos can seek out opportunities in countries where you don't have any agents or salespeople of your own.

The Role of the Nakodo

Nakodos can perform a number of roles in international marketing, all with the ultimate goal of bringing together buyers and sellers, consummating business deals, and earning commissions. Nakodos are effective for short-term, specific sales opportunities, poor on long-term promotion.

A nakodo usually starts from the buyer's side: he or she looks for a supplier to meet a specific product need, as was the case with Larry Dorsett. A buyer expresses a need, the nakodo finds a supplier. In this situation you, the supplier, may be competing with other firms approached by the nakodo. Eventually the nakodo will deal with the supplier who offers the best product, the best prices, the best commission, *and who seems most likely to live up to the agreement made with the nakodo.*

A nakodo may on occasion start from your—the supplier's—side, and actively promote your product. This approach is not very popular, because experienced nakodos have learned that it is easier to find a product to meet a need than to find a buyer for a particular product.

"It takes too much of my time to promote a specific line," says a friend of mine in Bogota, a veteran nakodo. "I could be spinning my wheels selling the wrong product. I prefer to look for a supplier once I have a live and ready buyer."

Promoting a line can also be risky. A nakodo never knows when a supplier will replace its international marketing manager, wiping out whatever agreements may have been made. Most nakodo deals are made on trust and a handshake. But even when things are put down in writing there is always a way out.

At the local level nakodos work well with friends and relatives who have their own businesses.

Nakodos can, and often do, help manufacturers build up international networks of agents. This is more of a consulting than a match-making function. It is not the sort of work nakodos are thrilled about because commission arrangements can be shaky. Say I introduce you to an agent in Australia. You may gladly pay me a commission on the agent's initial purchases, but how long will it take you to start making faces every time you have to send me a check? This type of work should be done on a fee basis. The same goes for licensing or joint-venture agreements. In any of these situations it takes time for business to develop. Usually suppliers prefer to pay commissions in the early stages, when the volume of business is still low, and cut out nakodos when bigger sales start materializing two or three years down the line.

The type of nakodo I am talking about is not a big-name, pricey, match-making consultant. My version of the nakodo is a self-supporting individual whose best role is to broker a straight buy-and-sell situation involving a tangible product. Essentially the nakodo is a lone operator with good connections, quick to respond to opportunities, ready to help cut red tape. The nakodo is the antithesis of a bureaucrat, usually looks at the bright side of a deal, and refuses to be discouraged by problems.

Here's the story of a nakodo who walked the extra mile to make sure everything was done right.

Bill Chan, a nakodo based in Hong Kong, contacts Energy Simulations, Inc., in Chicago after a trip to Beijing and passes on a lead from a hot prospect in China. Within ten days the Chinese end user issues an order for two demonstrator units to be shipped immediately by air.

The day of the shipment, Energy Simulations telexes Bill Chan that "the units have been turned over to our freight forwarders, Speedy Cargo." Missing from the telex: airway bill number, airline and flight number, expected date of arrival in Beijing, other vital information.

Bill, who works out of his apartment in Kowloon and keeps his telex in his living room, glances at his watch: 5:05 p.m. in Chicago. It's Friday. He can't wait two days for the information. He phones Energy Simulations; a security guard answers. "Sorry, there's nobody in the office. They all went home at 5."

"Unreal," Bill mutters. "Five minutes and they've scattered! What do they do, line up and wait for the bell like horses at the starting gate?"

Undaunted, Bill places a phone call to Speedy Cargo at O'Hare International Airport, finds out that nobody has told them the shipment was urgent or even bothered to book cargo space in advance. The shipment is wait-listed. All cargo space to Beijing is fully booked for ten days. After fifteen minutes of checking routing options, a cooperative dispatcher at Speedy Cargo books the shipment on a Lufthansa flight leaving the following morning for Frankfurt, with immediate transfer to a Frankfurt-Beijing flight. The shipment arrives on Monday, in time for an important demonstration, no thanks to the sloppy logistics of the manufacturer.

This sort of thing happens all the time. To a manufacturer, a nakodo order is just another piece of business. Perhaps nothing to get really excited about. To the nakodo each deal is important and urgent. A good nakodo will bend over backwards to make sure that nothing goes wrong.

Don't expect a nakodo to put on a long, sustained promotional effort. The nakodo has to eat and cannot afford to wait for results next year.

Long-term promotion and selling is best done by your own sales force. A nakodo who operates for a local agent may do little more than introduce key buyers.

Listen to and encourage nakodos who bring you business opportunities. *Your own sales force and agents cannot be everywhere.*

How to Find a Nakodo

Nakodos come to you when they have buyers for your type of product. Your first concern, therefore, is to listen with an open mind to what they have to say, and to be prepared to work with them on the deals they bring you.

Even if you have an international network of exclusive agents you still can and should encourage nakodos. Nakodos, however, are reluctant to approach large companies for fear of being turned away and looked down upon. Frankly, I don't blame them. Some of today's massive industrial bureaucracies, particularly in Europe, are totally incapable of dealing with a nakodo. First, because it is against "company policy"; second, because no individual has the guts, inclination, or authority to make decisions; third, because nothing gets done without going through several meetings.

Small and medium-size companies are easier to deal with, as are newcomers who have not been in international marketing long enough to straitjacket their operations into tight regulations.

You can do a number of things to find nakodos, but try in all cases to be discreet, tactful, and low-key.

1. *Use in-house links.*   The same people who may help you find overseas intelligence sources should be able to put you in touch with nakodos. Have them send catalogs and company information to friends and relatives abroad, to make them aware that you are approachable.

2. *Let overseas embassies and associations know.*   As you and your field managers travel around the world, drop in on commercial officers at embassies and associations, leave catalogs and business cards, encourage people to pass the word. Embassy and association personnel are always in touch with local business persons and professionals. Wherever there is a commercial library, make sure there is at least a complete set of your catalogs, and information on how someone can get in touch with your international marketing office.

3. *Call on academics, consultants, and researchers.*   Once again, here is an important group of professionals worth cultivating. Many of them will have knowledge of projects and opportunities and may put you on to a

nakodo (more likely, they will quietly suggest to a nakodo that he or she contact you).

The academic world should yield some of your best nakodos. Professors at universities and polytechnics around the world are becoming more practical about the pursuit of business—an activity which does not have to conflict with their academic duties.

4. *Keep your eyes and ears open.*   Anybody who may have access to a buyer for your product is a potential nakodo. You will find nakodos in the most unexpected places, not only when you travel but also among your social and business contacts back home.

Not all nakodos are local. An international nakodo, for instance, is one who travels extensively throughout the world or in a major area. Someone, in other words, like Larry Dorsett, whose line of business is different from yours but who may come in contact with people who could be prospects for your product. If you sell electronic components, don't turn your back on an international carpet salesperson next time you go to a party. You may be ignoring a useful nakodo! Let Larry Dorsett jot down your name, phone, and telex in his little black book. You might hear from him when you least expect it.

Let people know that you have a positive, cooperative, accommodating attitude and that any legitimate business opportunity brought your way will be rewarded. Encourage your branch and regional offices to cultivate nakodos as well.

How to Evaluate a Nakodo

When is a nakodo lead for real? How do you avoid wasting time on nebulous deals?

First, you simply cannot avoid wasting time. This is part of the international marketing game—or any selling game. Second, many deals will be nebulous, but can you take any chances? How nice it would be if we could. sail through a business career jumping from one sure deal to another! But even when a nakodo brings you ten deals and they all fizzle out you can't cut him or her off. You could make a killing on the eleventh!

Blind trust in a nakodo is not what I am talking about. There are nakodos, and then there are nakodos. Establish their credibility early. When you are reasonably sure of a nakodo's connections and seriousness, don't worry too much about wasting time. Sooner or later the connection may pay off.

But when a nakodo casts about indiscriminately for business opportunities, you are better off setting down some basic rules or dropping the connection entirely.

The rules are simple.

1. *Work with nakodos who are specific and selective.*   Beware of nakodos who on Monday want an urgent quotation for plastic car seat covers and on Tuesday have a sizzling deal for hospital beds. In most cases they are merely collecting public bid requests already well known to everybody in the bazaar.

2. *Aim nakodos at their best targets.*   Since the main value of nakodos is to dig up specific sales, you must find out exactly where they have their best connections. If a nakodo rubs elbows with top officials at the Ministry of Agriculture, don't ask him or her to go looking for business in the Ministry of Telecommunications.

3. *Ask for details.*   Vague nakodo requests for quotations, such as, "Need full information on air-conditioners," are useless and give you legitimate grounds to question a nakodo's credibility. Nakodos who can send you details such as size, weight, power, model, application, quantity, and other specifications, without being asked, show at least an understanding of common business sense. Hang on to them!

4. *Be leery of public bids.*   The best nakodo deals are those which you can negotiate with the end user. This implies access to "the right people" and knowledge of a project which your competition may not be aware of. On public competitive bids, nakodos can prove the value of their connections by alerting you to projects well before they are announced to the public. Nakodos who tell you about a project after it has been announced are not doing you any favors.

5. *Be leery of urgent deals.*   Nakodos who desperately need quotations by next Friday are also suspect. Where have they been? What happened to their inside sources and influential friends?

How to Work with a Nakodo

The best nakodo deals are one-time sales with clearly spelled out commissions and terms. Ongoing, open-ended agreements are less likely to yield results. For one thing, the nakodo may quickly lose interest. For another, responsibility for sustained promotion is up to your salespeople and agents.

Deal with nakodos discreetly. Keep a low profile and tight lips. There's no need to brag about your connections and exploits. Your nakodos should also do their thing quietly and efficiently. You don't want an army of irregulars setting the countryside on fire, calling attention to themselves and messing up the work of your agents and salespeople.

The less people know about your "irregulars," the more difficult it will be for the competition to assess your real sales power.

When a nakodo approaches you out of the blue, without any prior contact, try to estimate his or her credibility. Apply the five basic rules we just looked at, but always be positive. Don't put the nakodo through an impossible obstacle course.

Who should deal with nakodos? This depends on your product. If you manufacture computerized industrial security systems, nakodos should work directly with your international marketing division. If you manufacture office copiers, nakodos should get in touch with your local field manager, salesperson, or agent—unless the deal is unusually large and important.

As in other phases of international marketing, you will have to play it by ear, case by case. The important thing is to encourage everybody in your network, including agents, to be receptive to nakodo feelers.

When you are satisfied that a nakodo is reasonably reliable, keep him or her supplied with promotional material, basic pricing information, and product specifications. The more questions the nakodo can ask a potential buyer, the more specific the lead, the easier your job in evaluating the situation.

Face-to-face meetings with nakodos are imperative. There is no other way to develop a close relationship. A name on a telex, a voice on the telephone, are not enough. The best nakodo deals are based on mutual trust and understanding between a nakodo and the supplier. Meet your nakodos often!

Since nakodos are independent and will "work" for you only when they have specific deals, there is little you can do about really running them. They are under no obligation to you. Keep it this way. Remember that nakodos are not agents. Their main assets are connections, freedom, and mobility.

Wherever you have branch and regional offices, local nakodo networks should be developed, cultivated, run, and paid by their managers.

The Nakodo versus the Agent

How do you operate nakodos and authorized agents under the same umbrella?

You can encourage nakodos in countries where you don't have authorized agents—low-priority countries which you have decided to keep on the back burner but where you will be happy to take whatever business you can get. Some of these nakodos could eventually make good permanent agents.

In countries where your agents are nonexclusive, use nakodos to build up direct sales if your authorized agents are not living up to what you expected. Sooner or later you may want to set up your own full-time sales office and hire nakodos who were particularly effective.

You can also turn over nakodo deals to agents, to help stimulate their sales or as a bonus (make sure you live up to your obligation to the nakodo!). This is good for morale; it shows agents that your aim is to support them rather than work against them. It gives you strength and stature in the market.

In priority markets where you have exclusive authorized agents, treat nakodo business with extreme tact. Poor agents will not be encouraged to do better if they know you are soliciting sales behind their backs. Good agents have every right to be incensed. The reason for working with nakodos in priority, exclusive markets is to back your agents to the hilt, not to work against them.

If yours is a high-value product, you should deal with the nakodo directly, but make sure you consult the agent. You don't want to develop a nakodo deal that the agent already knows about. This calls for tactful evaluation on your part. Try to get enough details from the nakodo—at least enough so that you and the agent can decide if this is a new, legitimate deal.

No nakodo will ever tell you everything about a deal unless he or she has enough trust in you. There is a limit to what you can ask. But you can try to find out, for instance, if the deal is in a province or market sector where your agent has not been active, the possible size of the business, which of your specific products and models are involved. The reason for these questions is not to learn who is the buyer and steal the sale from the nakodo, but to see if the project is similar to one the agent may be working on. If it is, there could be duplication of effort and everybody may have to put their cards on the table.

Nakodos who approach you, the international supplier or manufacturer, don't mix well with local agents. Tell nakodos to take their business to your agents and more than likely they will go instead to one of your competitors. Nakodos don't like manufacturers who refuse to get involved. They often suspect agents of being jealous and uncooperative. Agents should cultivate their own nakodos.

A nakodo who approaches an international supplier directly is not eager to work with an agent.

A U.S. manufacturer of computer-based training systems was contacted by a nakodo with access to a large industrial group in Italy. The manufacturer's international marketing manager didn't show the slightest interest.

"Go talk to our agent in Milan," he said.

"I prefer to deal with you," the nakodo insisted. "You can protect your Italian agents; I fully understand that. But my clients are a very large company, your agent has not contacted them, and I will only work with you directly."

"Sorry, we can't," the U.S. executive replied, making no attempt to seek a compromise or at least to keep the contact live.

The nakodo went to another U.S. firm, which quickly agreed to pursue a deal that led to a $1 million contract.

Encourage nakodos and convince your agents that every effort you make to promote the product and stimulate leads will only result in more sales and profits for them. The way to prove it is to play it straight, letting them profit from all nakodo deals.

To avoid the risk of losing your nakodos when your authorized agents are involved, monitor all deals and make sure that nobody tries to pull a fast one down the line. It takes time and effort, but if the result is bigger sales, it's worth it!

How to Pay a Nakodo

How much, when, and how you pay nakodos has everything to do with how they relate to you and whether they will ever want to deal with you again. If a nakodo brings you a good deal, do everything you can to encourage repeat business.

You can pay a nakodo a fixed fee or a commission. Commissions are more interesting to both sides. Fees can lead to tears and regrets—they can turn out to be minuscule in relation to the size of the final order, or too high, causing the supplier to moan and groan about costs and losses.

Here are some suggestions about nakodo commissions.

1. *Commissions to nakodos are legitimate.* Get rid of the notion that paying commissions to someone outside the company is unclean. Many independent consultants collect fat fees from firms that would never condescend to set aside a percentage to a nakodo. The irony is that consultants at best will do some terrain reconnaissance. They never bring you specific orders. A nakodo always points you to a live target—a possible sale. Be happy when you have to pay a nakodo commission!

2. *Pay promptly.* Nakodos are independent. They have business and living expenses. The longer you delay paying them, the more you alienate

them. Salaried executives and staff in large corporations are often insensitive to the problems of independent business people with no guaranteed income. Companies that unjustly retain nakodo commissions for months are a dime a dozen.

Play games with nakodos' commissions and they will soon tear your name out of their little black books. A nakodo's commission should be on its way twenty-four hours after you have been paid. Don't keep it. It's not your money!

3. *Live up to your word.*   An easy principle, yet one which is broken all the time. If you are going to gripe when it's time to pay a nakodo the 10 percent you agreed on, don't make a 10 percent deal to begin with. Make a deal and stick to it.

There are suppliers who try to work nakodo deals with no fixed percentage: "Play ball with us and if the deal comes through we'll take care of you." Perhaps because yours is a big-name corporation, the nakodo is impressed and agrees to play ball. Later the person who made the promises acts dumb and helpless ("I thought I could get the executive committee to go along with it") or brushes you off ("Well, it turned out our field reps already knew about the project").

Most nakodos I have met over the years have fallen once for the "we'll take care of you" trap. A basic rule among nakodos is that the larger the supplier, the shakier the agreement. Do your international marketing executives have authority to make deals with outsiders? Or, if they do and later you go back on the deal, will they claim that the matter is entirely out of their hands?

The smaller your company and the more authority your executives have to make decisions, the easier it will be for you to work with and benefit from nakodo connections.

4. *Don't be stingy.*   Make a deal with a nakodo at a commission rate attractive to him or her, and one you can live with. In most cases it will be from 5 to 10 percent.

If the nakodo needs more, be understanding. Suppliers like to talk about "finders' fees" to describe nakodo commissions. This is misleading and somewhat insulting, because it implies that all a nakodo does is slip you the name of a buyer, sit back, and wait for the money.

Nakodos have expenses and obligations. If they ask you for 15 percent, there may be legitimate reasons. If the deal is likely to take six months to come to life, the nakodo will have expenses—entertainment, travel, telex, telephone—which you would have to absorb if the deal were being worked by one of your salespeople.

In some situations a nakodo should be happy with 2 or 3 percent, such as on a multimillion-dollar sale, or one which will take little time, effort, and money.

After a deal is made, don't try to chisel nickels and dimes out of the nakodo's commission. This is dishonest, unfair, and makes a supplier look cheap. Some of them don't seem to mind, as my friend Pieter Van Der Jong can tell you.

Pieter found a project for two prefabricated clinics in Saudi Arabia and made a deal with a British supplier to do the job. It wasn't an easy project. Engineers had to fly to Riyadh fifteen times, layouts and specifications were changed every three weeks. But eventually the order was confirmed and the project completed.

When commission time arrived, Pieter was told not to worry. There had been some delays, but his check would soon be in the mail. "Soon" became weeks. Pieter's telexes and phone calls to the company got nastier. In the end he got an unbelievable recitation of excuses: the project had taken longer than expected; travel expenses went beyond the original budget; the contract was made in Saudi riyals and since then the British pound had risen, resulting in a foreign exchange loss to the company; management wished they hadn't gotten into the contract in the first place; actually Mr. Blake, "our director whom you dealt with, is no longer with us" and never properly informed management.

Pieter was fit to be tied, knowing full well that behind all the whining and sobbing was a fair profit. Besides, a deal was a deal, and Pieter himself had had unusual expenses in helping to grease the wheels. A settlement was finally reached, giving Pieter a commission which amounted to a fraction of what he was entitled to.

For this shoddy performance, the manufacturer ended up on Pieter's black list—nothing calamitous, although there is such a thing as a nakodo grapevine which sooner or later picks up all the latest gossip. No need to say anything about where Pieter will *not* go next time he runs into a similar project!

5. *Protect your agents.*   You have an obligation to protect your nakodos, and, above all, an obligation to protect your agents. Include in all nakodo deals a profit for your agents, even when you are working with the nakodo directly. If your agents are not exclusive, the profit can be used as a bonus, as we saw.

6. *Spell it out.*   Protect yourself and the nakodo: lay down the exact terms of a deal. In addition to the specific commission rate, there are four important elements.

First, the value of the sale. This is the total amount of the order less some allowable deductions. The most common ones are freight, insurance, installation charges, operator training, and the translation of maintenance manuals. You can deduct them from the total amount of the order *before* figuring out the nakodo's commission.

You should *not* deduct the amount of any commissions or profits you want to set aside for your agent. This is your responsibility, not the nakodo's.

Second, the terms of payment. The nakodo should be paid as you collect your money. For instance, if the order includes designing a facility (such as a clinic or a school), and the buyer makes a partial payment when you deliver the design, you should immediately pass on to the nakodo his or her share of the partial payment. The only time a supplier is justified in retaining a nakodo's commission until the entire project has been concluded is when there is a possibility some of the money may have to be returned to the end user. This is extremely rare in international marketing, if you insist on being paid by irrevocable and confirmed letter of credit—as most smart companies do.

Third, the nakodo's obligations to others. The nakodo may have to share the commission with an assistant, partner, or friend. This is not your business, unless the nakodo asks you to handle the payment to the third party, and this is both legal and ethical. You will then have to adjust the nakodo's net commission accordingly.

Fourth, expenses, profits, and losses. Some suppliers try to offer a nakodo a percentage of the profit instead of the total value of the sale. This is dandy for the supplier. All sorts of expenses can be claimed (as in the example we just saw), which the nakodo will be powerless to dispute. To avoid this, experienced nakodos will ask you to stipulate that you will live up to the agreement regardless of your final profit or loss. If you cannot swallow this, take another look at the commission rate and try to settle for something lower.

Whatever you arrive at, spell it out in writing!

7. *Don't ask!* Whatever a nakodo does with his or her commission is none of your business. Do you ask your agents how they are going to spend their profits? How much they are going to pay their salespeople? Who they are going to take out to lunch? Treat nakodos the same way. Their commission is their business. Don't ask!

Can You Trust a Nakodo?

Trust is mutual. If you play games with nakodos, don't expect them to be loyal. Nakodos are loners who have to cover themselves because nobody else will do it for them. The nakodo has two concerns: to find a reliable and trustworthy supplier, and to get the order.

We've discussed stingy, inconsiderate, insensitive, and dishonest suppliers. Be realistic. Assume that a nakodo will think the worst of you until you prove otherwise. It is up to you to sell your company's credibility. If you succeed, you've won half the battle. There is still the question of whether your offer is competitive—in price, specifications, features, delivery, terms. Nakodos will try to give themselves a break by seeking more than one offer. It is a matter of *loyalty to themselves*.

If you have agreed to protect the nakodo and expect mutual exclusivity, you are asking the nakodo to place all bets on you. The nakodo may agree, but the decisive test is whether the nakodo wants to work with you on more than today's sale. This depends on four *ifs*:

1. If you offer the nakodo a good deal.

2. If you convince the nakodo of your credibility.

3. If your prices, product, and conditions are competitive.

4. If there are repeat opportunities.

Establish these four points and you will be on your way to creating nakodo trust.

Best Nakodo Territories

You can find nakodos everywhere. In every country there are independent business people who will broker sales by finding buyers or suppliers, even in structured, complex markets like the Scandinavian countries, West Germany, Switzerland, Canada, and the United States. In these countries nakodos may be difficult to find. Your best opportunities will be to cultivate consultants and professionals in your industry.

Nakodos work best and are easiest to find in countries where business is not rigidly channeled into well-defined marketing patterns. They excel where they can roam far afield, where personal connections are helpful and important, where local regulations and customs are so complex and exasperating that a supplier will gratefully embrace anyone who knows how to get things untangled.

The best nakodo territories include the Middle East, Africa, Latin America, south and southeast Asia—particularly expanding new countries with money for big projects and to equip local industry.

In these areas, even if they don't include your top priority markets, try to develop and support local nakodos, especially where it would be too expensive to seek out and establish agents or your own salespeople.

Don't stay away from a country simply because local rules and regulations are too complicated or difficult. Chances are this will discourage most of your competitors—leaving the field fairly open for you.

Who Needs Them?

Every manufacturer, supplier, and agent can use nakodos. Find them, welcome them, cultivate them, use them, profit from them. They cost you nothing. Start collecting nakodos today.

8

Hidden Talents

Charles Nguyen has a 9-to-5 job as a stockroom clerk at the Zeus Corporation warehouse in Albany. Evenings, Charles puts in four hours as a bagger at one of the local 7-Elevens. Charles, a former official in the South Vietnamese Foreign Ministry, is fluent in English, French, and three Southeast Asian languages.

The Zeus Corporation, manufacturer of physics laboratory equipment, does a fair amount of business abroad—including Southeast Asia. Charles could, perhaps, be an asset to Zeus. But nobody in the international marketing department has ever heard of Charles Nguyen.

Why?

First, because Charles is a refugee, and many personnel departments still stick to the stereotype of a refugee as a semiliterate person who has to be taught from scratch.

Second, and more ominous, because the Zeus international marketing department does not have a talent bank and has never bothered to find out what human resources may lie right under its nose.

Are you aware of all the talents and skills within *your* company which could help your international business? Do *you* have a talent bank?

Because of the ease with which you can, thanks to the personal computer, collect, file, sort, update, and retrieve data, the talent bank can be a weapon of immense power and effectiveness in international marketing. If you don't have one, reach for your computer and start building one without wasting another day.

What do you really know about your own employees? What can they contribute to international marketing? Hiring usually means finding people to fill vacancies. With a live databank, however, you can pinpoint individual skills and strengths, and then decide how best to use them.

The international talent bank draws on personnel records to extract information about employees, but it also relies on other sources to develop information on talented individuals, including outsiders, who could contribute today or tomorrow to your international sales.

The big difference between employee records and a talent bank is that one is merely a cold file on individuals, while the other is a live, constantly updated weapon of international marketing.

The purpose of an international talent bank is to know which talents within and outside the company could contribute to the success of international marketing.

Talent banks should be created not only in your international marketing office but wherever you have a local or regional operation.

RDF Personnel

One of the most vital tasks of your talent bank is to pinpoint people with sales experience or skills, to serve in your rapid deployment sales force. To help you build up reserves for your RDF, open also a file on every salesperson in your domestic sales division. You may need them in an emergency.

If you run into an unusually attractive opportunity abroad, need someone to jump into it and all your RDF people are busy elsewhere, get help from domestic sales. Domestic salespeople may not know the capital of Ecuador (why should they?), but at least they know the product and the company.

Domestic sales managers will rant and rave if anybody dares lay a finger on their protégés. It is up to management to make the company's *entire* marketing operation work as a team and not as in-house rivals. The concept of flexible sales power works both ways. At times, domestic will need to borrow people from international, and international should be ready to pitch in. The goal is to try not to waste any sales opportunities.

You may have a number of experienced salespeople hidden in jobs not related to sales. Perhaps when they came looking for jobs, there were no openings in sales, and they took something else. Unfortunately, once new employees are hired, their job applications are unlikely to be aired often, and whoever did the interviewing may quickly forget their special talents. Unless an employee actively seeks promotion or transfer to the sales department, nobody else may lift a finger.

Earlier we saw the importance of putting as many people "on the line" as possible. Even if your budget does not allow you to make full use of your in-house sales talents right away, identify qualified people, train them, hold them in reserve and ready, give them support jobs in the office. You will be glad to have reserve manpower to deploy rapidly, without depleting your forces in other markets. This task is impossible without a thorough and continuing assessment of your in-house sales talents.

The importance of a ready reserve is vital if you have started to penetrate some of the world's largest markets. Your initial marketing efforts in

West Germany may have been tough going, but suddenly you find doors beginning to open, resistance easing up. Can you quickly send in two, three, or four additional, well-trained salespeople to reinforce your patient field manager?

Other Useful Talents

Experience in selling is a priority talent but not the only one that can contribute to international marketing. Furthermore, if someone is hired to run the postage meter and the office copier, this does not mean the person has nothing else to offer! We've already seen the types of personal talents and backgrounds that can sharpen your international operations. Let's review them.

1. *Foreign languages.*   Next to sales this is one of the more obvious skills in international marketing. Find out which employees speak, read, write, or at least understand a foreign language. Make an estimate of the person's fluency and background. A native speaker is not necessarily a good correspondent or translator, but he or she can make an excellent interpreter. You need interpreters to deal with visitors. You also need translators to help with correspondence, foreign language brochures, and maintenance manuals. If any of your linguists is potential sales force material, so much the better.

2. *Overseas contacts.*   Which employees have friends and relatives abroad? Focus on friends more than families—people with similar interests, training and background. The contacts may be good intelligence sources or nakodos. If you are an agent, concentrate on people who have connections in countries where major suppliers in your industry are located.

3. *Foreign residence.*   Find out which employees have lived abroad, what they did, what they know about foreign countries. In addition to language skills they can contribute opinions and advice on how to approach markets, end users, agents, and give you valuable pointers on travel. They may come in handy when you need to send temporary administrative or technical staff abroad.

4. *Cultural background.*   Residence abroad is one way to learn about the rest of the world. Another is an interest or background in history, cultures, religions. An employee whose hobby is Buddhism may not make a tangible contribution to your sales in Thailand but could provide useful background to keep your salespeople in the area from making fools of themselves. Use this type of person in briefing sessions.

5. *Negotiating skills.*   You are likely to find these skills among senior and junior executives, personnel and labor relations officers. Make an assessment of their actual experience and how it might apply in an international situation, such as negotiating a licensing agreement or a turnkey project.

6. *Tact and diplomacy.*   This is more of an art than a skill. You will need diplomats to keep lines of communications open in markets where for the time being you don't need or cannot use a salesperson. Look for diplomats among your company's executives, simply because of the prestige of their titles.

In assessing executives and other possible diplomats, you will have to rely on personal impressions. If your company's executive vice-president is taking a long holiday trip through South Asia, don't ask him or her to drop in on the Minister of Education of the various countries unless you are reasonably sure the person will make a good impression. Not all high-level executives are polished diplomats!

7. *Photography.*   Here is a skill not used enough in international marketing, and I am not talking about fuzzy snapshots of agents, spouses, and salespersons around a dinner table in Athens. Good, professional-quality photos or videos of overseas installations, demonstrations, agents' facilities, sales training sessions, displays, trade fair exhibits, and other events can be invaluable in helping you promote sales in other markets.

Find out which employees in your company are handy with a camera, send them out on occasion with field managers or salespeople. This is cheaper than hiring outside professionals, you encourage in-house talents, and you promote a "think global!" concept within the company.

If you are an agent, anybody on your staff who has media skills will be an asset not only to you but also to the suppliers you represent. Make sure your suppliers know about this "extra service" you can offer them to help promote their sales around the world.

8. *Technical troubleshooting.*   Do you have any technicians or engineers on your staff who speak a foreign language, have lived or were born abroad? Keep them on tap. Use them next time you have to send someone abroad to make an installation, train local technicians, or do maintenance work.

The Opposition's Talents

Building files on individuals who work for the competition is as vital as creating your own in-house talent bank. Don't just look at them as the enemy. Look at them also as potential recruits for your own sales forces.

Take a good agent or salesperson away from a competitor and you will strike a double blow for your side.

Before you try to turn any of the opposition's people, you have to know who they are, where they come from, what they do, where they operate, how successful they are, what are their favorite tactics and special talents, how much they are paid.

Information about men and women in the competition should go into your talent bank. If you are like most people in international marketing, your talent bank on the competition is probably a fistful of business cards held together with a rubber band and tucked in the main drawer of your desk or in the plastic sleeves of a pocket-size wallet. References to specific individuals may occasionally appear in reports from your field managers and salespeople, invariably as incidental comments in a sales or travel report.

Go for the people who are out selling—field managers and salespeople. A competitor's success may have a lot to do with the brilliant strategies of an international marketing manager, but in the final crunch it's the men and women in the field who face the music and make a difference. A manager promoted from the front lines may have lost some of his or her punch. People in the field *today*, facing competition and producing sales, should be prime candidates for your recruiting efforts.

As you collect and evaluate data on the competition, look for specific talents and skills—sales performance, along with knowledge of languages, cultural background, tact, and all the other desirable qualities that you look for among your own personnel.

Nakodo Talents

Up-to-date files on nakodos are indispensable. Not only of the good ones who put you on to successful deals, but also of the ones who never got you anywhere and whose abilities and connections may be suspect. The information in one case may help you expand your sales, in the other avoid wasting time.

A file on a nakodo will let you assess his or her reliability when a new sales opportunity comes up. It can also help when you initiate a deal and seek a nakodo to help you get the order. For instance, you hear of a possible project in the Ministry of Health in Jordan, a country where you have no salespeople or agents. Your talent bank tells you that two years ago in Amman you met someone who claimed to have good local connections. You never exchanged letters or telexes, but you were smart enough to open a file on this potential "irregular." You have nothing to lose, so you contact the nakodo. It certainly is worth a try.

Talents in Reserve

Outsiders other than competitors have talents which can be translated into higher sales abroad. Keep them in mind for full-time or for specific short-term assignments in marketing, intelligence gathering, promotion, public relations, or any other phase of your international operations.

Whenever you meet a consultant or advisor, for instance, try to pinpoint the person's particular expertise, background, and connections. A traveling salesperson who sits next to you on a flight from Lagos to Nairobi may be in an entirely different line of business, but his or her knowledge of Nigeria, Ghana, Liberia, and Senegal may be just what you will need next year.

Keep track also of the talents and skills of VIPs and end users. What do they do? Whom do they know? What do they know?

In short, the international talent bank is not a duplicate of your company's personnel records. It is a live and useful file of in-house and outside talents which can be used in your international operations.

Running the Talent Bank

The international talent bank is the responsibility of the person in charge of international marketing and sales; he or she must be accessible quickly, easily, at any time.

The personnel manager may not take kindly to the idea of "turning over" records to marketing. Or to letting marketing comb through personnel files to earmark individuals with special skills. This has to be firmly straightened out by management. Everybody is on the same side. The alternative is to cause unnecessary delays and eventually kill the talent bank as a live marketing weapon.

Running a talent bank to support a policy of tactical, flexible international marketing can create some disruptions in other departments in the company. An international marketing manager on the prowl for hidden talents, likely to want to steal or borrow people from other jobs, is bound to make waves.

The point has to be drilled into all managers that the company must try to make the fullest and best use of its human resources—whether in international marketing or in the mailroom—and that some wave-making is stimulating and healthy.

All managers should cooperate in the continuous assessment of personnel, and this includes helping the international marketing manager pinpoint people with particular talents for overseas sales expansion. Furthermore, if the goal is to make optimum use of personnel, shifting people to international marketing does not necessarily mean that they have to be replaced at their old jobs.

The process of human resource evaluation applies also whenever a new employee is hired, for whatever job. Let the international marketing manager know, and give him or her an opportunity to interview and evaluate the employee.

How to Set up a Talent Bank

Draw up a roster of the talents you can use to promote your international business. In addition to the basic ones such as sales experience, include those uniquely related to your product and its applications. For instance, if you sell chemistry lab equipment, anybody on your staff with a good background in chemistry, such as teaching, can be useful in overseas presentations, teacher-training seminars, and trade exhibits.

Relate the roster of talents to your needs in specific countries. You may need diplomats in Brazil, Nigeria, Pakistan, and the Philippines; a photographer to shoot videos of your latest installations in Australia and Kenya; a Spanish-speaking technician for a special presentation to key end users in Argentina.

Some of these needs are immediate and one-time. Others are continuous and not related to just a few countries. Always keep the roster updated and handy. Enter it in a computer file which you can access quickly.

To evaluate your own personnel, you may have to change your job application questionnaire. Most forms cover some of the qualifications we have discussed. Knowledge of foreign languages is one, but there is seldom an attempt to assess the person's fluency in the language. The usual questionnaire does not ask if you lived abroad, where, for what purpose, and for how long.

In your new questionnaire include whatever talents and skills can help you boost your international sales and profits. You need not go into exhausting detail. It is enough to identify people who may have something to contribute. Follow up with a personal interview for more details. If you create a new questionnaire, make sure all your existing personnel fill it out, unless yours is a small company and you can talk to people one by one.

When you create files on people from the competition, you obviously won't be passing out questionnaires. Enlist the help of field managers, salespeople, and agents. The gist of your file on a competitor is sales results. How successfully or poorly is the person performing? How long has he or she been at the job? What main successes can be attributed to the individual? The main purpose of your talent bank on the competition is to identify individuals who may one day be willing to shift to your side.

Talent bank information can be entered and stored in different ways. Don't rely on a little black book. Use a computer. There is no reason for even the smallest international marketing operation not to have one. Factual information which can be condensed to single words or yes/no entries can be stored in a databank management system. Set up "fields" for the specific talents and skills you are looking for. For instance:

Languages

Foreign residence

Contacts abroad

Through the databank you can zero in on individuals by sorting and sifting information by fields. If you are looking for specific language skills, you can break down the "language" field. Create fields for Arabic, Spanish, Portuguese, and Japanese, if your priority markets are Saudi Arabia, Spain, Portugal, Venezuela, and Japan.

Keep the fields down to a reasonable number—say, under fifteen. Otherwise the files become too clumsy to handle. Essentially the databank is an index, from which you go to individual files for more detail. Individual files can be kept with a word processing program. Expand on the details you entered in the databank. Use the narrative approach, with tight editing.

Try to limit the information on each person to less than two pages. Edit, edit, edit. Don't open a file unless you have something specific to say about an individual. Length and bulk are not important. Content is. Divide your files into at least two major sections: in-house personnel and outsiders.

Review your files frequently, particularly the ones on the competition. If you note unanswered questions, ask field managers and salespeople to help get the answers. Encourage field people to include in their reports the achievements or failures of individuals. If a competitor beats you to a deal, you need to know not only what were the price and conditions, but who in the competition masterminded the coup. This puts pressure on your field people to be more alert and inquisitive. It is too easy to brush off a sales defeat by claiming that "their price was lower." Pay special attention to talented people in the competition who would be assets to your own company if they switched over.

Nakodo files can be set up to show best market sectors, types of end users with which the nakodo is best connected, information on previous deals and contacts with the nakodo, which ones were converted into orders.

Opinions on the personalities and aptitudes of individuals—insiders or outsiders—can help you estimate where they can do you the most good in international marketing. There are two ways you can try to figure out what makes a person tick. One is through psychologists. Your company may already use them, full-time or part-time. It is not necessary for every employee to go through a session with a psychologist. Save it for those who seem to have interesting and useful talents.

The other way is through graphology. Many European firms require a handwritten cover letter with an employment application. Graphologists—also listed in telephone directories as handwriting analysts—are used regularly to screen job candidates or to help direct them to the job for which they are best suited. If your company has not yet discovered the value of handwriting analysis, use the technique at least in your international marketing department whenever you have pinpointed a talented or skillful person. All salespeople, including RDF members, should have some psychological testing, and their handwriting analyzed.

From psychologists and graphologists you will get unique insights on a person's dominant characteristics. Traits such as discretion, respect, sensitivity, general culture, intuitive-rational intelligence, sense of responsibility, understanding, tolerance, and trustworthiness—all of which are vital in international marketing—can be revealed through psychological and handwriting analysis.

The Talent Bank and the Agent

A talent bank is also a major asset to the agent. An agent can get information about local competition more quickly and thoroughly than an international marketing manager 6000 miles away. The movements of branch and agency managers and their salespeople can be followed with less effort, and an agent can also analyze the performance of field managers and salespeople who visit the country on behalf of competing suppliers. The evaluation, filing, storage, and retrieval principles we have discussed in this chapter can be applied by agents with minor changes when creating their own talent banks.

Keep It Compact

One of the problems with a talent bank is that it may become too big eventually. The problem is common to all intelligence gathering. Yet you shouldn't lose track of important potential talents inside or outside your organization just for the sake of keeping things neat and compact. Constant review and editing are the only solution. You can also expand your basic "index" databank by adding fields that will help you narrow down your searches.

9

Ignorance Is Grief

How do international marketing salespeople learn their jobs? Usually by the seat of their pants. What passes for training focuses heavily on product knowledge and in-house order-handling procedures. Actual field conditions are glossed over.

The competition is dealt with lightly because "they couldn't touch us with a 10-foot pole," so why bother? In some firms, training and brainwashing are hard to distinguish. Their sales managers—domestic or international—sound more like cheerleaders than responsible executives concerned with giving their troops the straight facts about what they are likely to run into when they leave the safety of the home office. In international marketing this can be risky. The excitement of a high-pitched sales talk quickly wears thin when you are 10,000 miles away in a strange land, and you discover that your competitors aren't the weaklings they were portrayed to be! You wish someone had armed you with more live ammunition and less hoopla.

Brainwashing—intentional or not—is still the object of many international sales meetings. I am all for getting salespeople stirred up about their product and company. Keep up morale and enthusiasm; it can never be too high! But let's balance them with realistic training. Lessons on how to improve your salesmanship can be learned, up to a point, from crack domestic salespeople. You may like to trot them out at international meetings. This can be a good idea, but remind yourself that these men and women probably know nothing about what conditions are really like abroad.

In my one year of training in Sweden, prior to being sent to New York as a rookie salesman, I was taught by Stockholm salesmen all the tricks of how to demonstrate and sell our calculating machines. When I arrived in New York, I tried them all. Nothing worked! Nobody in Stockholm had prepared me for the objections I was going to butt my head against in New York! I don't think they really knew. Or perhaps they didn't want to deflate the enthusiasm of a new recruit.

Letting people learn by trial and error is a waste. Furthermore, there are lessons you never learn unless someone hits you over the head with them. Tactical, creative international marketing requires continuous training beyond mere product knowledge.

Who, in your company, needs training in international marketing?

1. Field managers and salespeople, including seasoned veterans

2. Recruits and reserve salespeople—your rapid-deployment force

3. International marketing support staff

4. Executives and staff in related departments

5. Everybody in the company (morale-boosting)

6. Agents, nakodos, intelligence sources

If you don't now have a systematic training program reaching these six groups, you're running a loose ship—you're falling behind!

The New Concept in Training

International marketing training must aim at making managers, salespeople, and support staff aware of how to develop strategies and tactics aimed at specific competitors and priority markets. Which is quite different from confining your training to sending rookie salespeople to clinics that teach general selling principles (not always applicable to your own product).

In the United States, firms such as General Motors, the Beatrice Corporation, and the Rolm Corporation are sending executives to business schools which offer customized management courses. Few firms, however, have international marketing staffs large enough to sustain special courses at business schools. Furthermore, an effective training program must take in virtually your entire personnel and not merely the people in charge of selling. The answer is to create in-house training programs tailor-made to your own needs. They should cover a wide range of topics, some traditional, some innovative. They must be flexible and easily adaptable to changing needs and conditions.

Your in-house training must also be two-way. Everybody—including executives—is a teacher *and* a student.

Training Sessions

The worst international sales meeting I ever attended was run by an electronics manufacturer whose executives for three days bombarded a roomful of overseas agents with statistics about how well the firm was doing in the *domestic* market, how bad and insignificant the competition was. There was plenty of hoopla, luncheons, cocktail receptions, speeches, and dinners. But the so-called training sessions were strictly one-way. None of the agents said a word. Nobody asked them to volunteer suggestions or even to describe market conditions in their own countries. They sat and listened and then went home having learned next to nothing.

My most useful international meeting was conducted by my first employer, the Swedish office machines manufacturer. They did do many things right! Salespeople and agents from thirty countries gathered in Saltsjobaden, a summer resort near Stockholm, for one week. There were few plenary sessions and speeches. Most of the time we worked in small groups, simulating sales situations, discussing specific competitors, trying to come up with practical selling techniques. Everybody participated, everybody learned.

Creative training should never stop, not even for seasoned field managers and salespeople. Nobody is ever sharp enough. A smug "supersalesperson" can easily develop a dull edge. Here are some principles to follow in setting up your training program.

1. Profit by everybody's experience and ideas. Every participant has something to contribute.

2. Schedule at least one two-hour session every two weeks. Two hours allows enough time to discuss several topics. Meeting more frequently than every two weeks can become a chore and an obligation.

3. Run your meetings on company time. Asking people to stay after hours is unfair. This is company business.

4. Concentrate on your sales force—field managers, salespeople, and your rapid-deployment force. Not all field people will be able to attend all sessions; some will be on the road. Include whoever is available, make sure that all participate at least fifteen or twenty times a year, set up special sessions when they are in town.

5. In all meetings include a blend of salespeople and support staff—an excellent way to make staff aware of field problems, and to encourage better solutions to order handling, shipping, and other procedures.

6. Invite any agents, intelligence sources, or nakodos who may be in town. These are unique opportunities to hear about real-life situations from the agents' side.

7. Bring in outside specialists from time to time for specific contributions, but keep them from delivering long-winded lectures.

8. Hold special sessions to train your rapid-deployment force and to keep them honed to cope with any sales situations which may surface in hot action zones. Remember, they are one of your strongest new weapons!

9. Keep the sessions lively; avoid repetitive routines. Always be specific, regardless of the topic. Focus on specific countries, specific competitors, specific situations.

10. Limit the sessions to ten or twelve people. If you have a larger staff, either rotate attendance (not everybody has to go to all meetings), or set up separate sessions.

11. Make sure everybody participates in discussions, and occasionally leads a session.

12. Invite people from other departments from time to time—including domestic sales.

13. Set up regular training sessions along these same principles, in every one of your overseas branch and regional offices. Encourage and help all agents to do the same.

Know Your Product

There is no excuse for international salespeople who don't know their product blindfolded. This has always been the foundation of all sales training. In spite of modern communications, a salesperson two continents away cannot always reach the home office for answers. Every day a prospect is left dangling is a loss of time and enthusiasm. It can cost you the order.

Your product and its features should be discussed at every training session. Product training is not always effective. You may lean too much on your "comprehensive" training manual—the one that covers every aspect of your product and every sales eventuality. The problem is that the thicker the manual, the less inclined people are to read it and absorb its contents.

Your rapid-deployment force should be particularly sharp on product and company know-how, because when you send them on a foreign assignment they probably will be dropped in the midst of a hot selling situation.

The Sales Pitch

Before you send your salespeople overseas, you may have enrolled them in one or more seminars where you are taught how to approach a prospect, how to handle objections, and how to close a sale. This is useful, but take it with a grain of salt. What works in Stockholm may not work in New York, remember?

In-house sessions on how to deal with agents and buyers overseas are more specific, practical, and realistic. Information and background for these sessions should come from your own field managers, salespeople, and outside specialists.

If you head an experienced, large international operation, you have already learned that there is no single selling technique that will work around the world. Differences between countries are too wide. Culture, religion, customs, and earning power are just a few of the aspects where no two countries are ever alike.

Motivation is another one. There may be a worldwide demand for your product, but the reasons people buy it are not always the same. This lesson has to be repeated to your sales force over and over again.

Let's say that in Germany your word processor appeals to office managers who want to save money; at current office wages it pays for itself in a year. In a developing country with low wages, where labor savings are not critical, office managers want your product to make up for the low educational level of office personnel. What sells your product in Saudi Arabia is that most of the people who use it are expatriate U.S., Canadian, and European office staff familiar with it in their own countries.

The key to creating your sales pitch *in each country*, therefore, is to spell out, as simply as possible, the paramount single reason why someone would buy your product. As you compare needs and motivation around the world, you will end up with several different answers. Discuss all of them at your international sales meetings and in training sessions. Train your salespeople to recognize differences in motivation and to know how to adapt their sales pitch accordingly.

Look also at the other side of the coin. Why, in each country, would someone *not* want to buy your product? This can be even more important than pinpointing positive motivation. You cannot get an order without successfully clearing all hurdles. Again, the answers will be different from one country to another and should be a valuable guide to salespeople in preparing their rebuttal to buyer objections.

Overseas selling technique also involves how to deal with people—tact, manners, and flexible thinking. For instance, success in business means different things to different people. For most business people in the United States, success means growth: bigger sales, bigger staffs, bigger profits. For many Europeans success is achieving and maintaining a comfortable level of sales and income. In Japan, loyalty and life-long service to a company also constitute success.

How a salesperson deals with a potential buyer, face to face, is the real test of your entire marketing effort. Fred Fireball may have been your crackerjack salesman back in Missouri, but if the first time he meets Joseph Leclerc, a big potential buyer in Brussels, he starts calling him Joe before they even have a chance to comment on the weather, Fred's skills may come to zilch.

No matter how many experts you bring in, you will never be able to absorb all the implications of cultural and other differences around the world. The best and most prudent approach is to train your field managers and salespeople to keep a low profile, avoid instant informality, and to be subdued in dress and manners.

Encourage your field people to be low-key in their presentations. You may have been taught to demonstrate your product with a flash of showmanship; your product may call for it. Make sure the approach is not offensive in the markets you are trying to conquer. In the long run, the most effective technique is to come across as a knowledgeable professional in full command of your product. If in doubt about a sales technique, check first with someone in the country itself—a consultant, an agent, an advertising or public relations firm—or, in your own country, with the country's embassy.

Constant review and sharpening of your sales pitch should be a priority topic at every training session, every international or regional sales meeting.

Training for Intelligence

Everybody in your company who may have contact with people abroad, particularly field managers and salespeople, should go through basic intelligence training and briefing. Although their main job is to sell, they should be alert at all times to any information that could benefit the company.

Basic rules of intelligence will be useful to salespeople also in their presentations, in handling buyer objections, and in their dealings with agents, VIPs, and other people they meet. Intelligence relies on tact and diplomacy—desirable traits in any international salesperson.

Here are some helpful rules which you can cover and enlarge upon at your training sessions.

1. *Don't be eager to introduce yourself.* When you first meet someone, let the conversation flow. Does it really make any difference in the beginning what your name is? Volunteering your name and other personal information could turn the other person off. In some countries this smacks of excessive familiarity and even an invasion of privacy, since you are forcing the other person to do the same.

2. *Ask, listen, and learn.* You cannot talk and learn at the same time. You already know what you are talking about. Your listener gains. All you

do is give out information—perhaps not to a competitor, but to someone who may later on pass it on to one. Can you take a chance? Instead, ask questions and encourage the other person to talk. The only way to really score is to come away with more information than you gave out.

3. *Don't rush to talk business.* You can't avoid talking about your work if someone asks you. In many countries, however, people will avoid prying into someone else's life and work, at least in the early stages of an acquaintance. In the long run you are better off trying to establish common interests and topics of conversation, building up to a relaxed relationship, especially if you expect to see the person again.

4. *Keep your voice down.* Speaking out loud is careless and foolish. Play it safe and assume that someome from the opposition may be within hearing distance: a field manager, a salesperson, an agent, a nakodo, an intelligence source, a friend, or an acquaintance! Assume also that others in your vicinity can understand everything you say. Once in a hotel dining room in Inner Mongolia I sat at a table next to a Brazilian who lived two blocks from the house where I was raised in Rio de Janeiro.

Another time, in the bus taking me from the airplane to the international arrivals building at Fiumicino airport in Rome, two salesmen for a well-known U.S. company loudly discussed how they would approach their Italian agents on Monday morning, what conditions they would insist on in their contract, and what other firms they would turn to if the agents didn't play ball.

Loose lips kill sales!

5. *Don't brag.* Bragging comes easily to many salespeople. Everybody likes to brag about their jobs, their families, their companies, their achievements, their personal connections, their travel experiences. There are more show-offs in the world than diplomats. Bragging, like talking too much, will benefit any competitor within hearing distance.

6. *Leave your badge in your room.* Don't wear a convention badge any longer than you have to. Perhaps you feel the "need to belong." All you accomplish is to advertise your presence and discourage people from opening up and talking. Take off your badge the moment you leave a convention or exhibit hall. Travel incognito!

7. *Don't seem eager for information.* The more intently you quiz someone, the more defensive they may become (unless they are the bragging type!). Be casual. If you have important questions to ask, scatter them among inoffensive, inocuous ones, and don't rush to jot things down in your notebook. Do it next time you go to the bathroom.

8. *Act savvy.* Without overdoing it, make it look as if you know more than you really do. This may encourage the other person to tell you things that he or she assumes are already common knowledge.

9. *Act dumb.* The opposite of being savvy also works. If you come across as an uninformed neophyte, wet behind your ears, you will often find eager talkers ready to enlighten you.

10. *Dangle some bait.* When you talk to competitors give out some information they may already know, or something not terribly important. Don't make up stories. Establish your credibility and make the other person loosen up. This can accomplish two things: the person may want to keep in touch with you in case you have more to divulge, or will contribute in return some useful bits of information. Either way you stand to gain.

11. *Hotel rooms are not soundproof.* Not only are walls paper-thin, but if you are making an international call and the connection is fuzzy, you are likely to raise your voice. Once in Riyadh I heard a competitor in the room next door give a blow-by-blow report on a pending project to his office in Chicago.

Know your Opposition

Knowing your opposition is another high-priority training subject. If you don't thoroughly understand the competition, you will never be able to develop effective sales pitches. Knowledge of markets is vital to any international operation, but your mission is to defeat the opposition.

How much do you and your sales force really know about your competitors? Do you view them with respect or discard them as harmless?

Gather all possible data on your competitors' products, pick out main features, advantages and disadvantages, why someone would buy, how much it costs. Look at them seriously and objectively. Remember, motivation and conditions change from country to country. Evaluate the competition's products the same way you evaluate yours: in terms of each specific country, especially your priority markets.

Discuss at your training sessions your competition's marketing, pricing, and promotional policies. Your salespeople and agents will contribute views and ideas on what each competitor is doing in specific markets around the world. Their reports will give you a unique opportunity to learn the day-to-day, front-line tactics of your competitors. Your worldwide success is the sum total of how well you respond to these tactics country by country. Go over them in every training session, set up discussions, encourage debate and devil's advocates. Focus on specific competitors; always be specific.

One of the best ways to learn about a competitor is to play with simulated scenarios—"What if?" situations. Relate them to specific countries where conditions are known. For instance: What if Tough Competitor X drops prices by 10 percent in Saudi Arabia? Switches agents in Brazil? Adds three salespeople to its international staff? Opens a branch in Melbourne? Appoints a wholesaler in Frankfurt? Starts marketing a cheaper made-in-Taiwan version of their bread-and-butter model? Sets up a regional office in Singapore?

Imagine a few bad situations and try to anticipate how to cope with them. This sort of game is not played often enough. Companies are afraid of calling attention to a competitor. Simulations can help give you a tactical edge over your competitors more effectively than anything else you may do in international marketing. The trick is to make them realistic and apply them to specific markets and conditions.

Another way simulations can be useful is to imagine unfavorable developments hitting specific countries, particularly your priority markets. For instance: What if Country A raises import duties on your product? What if the autocratic government of Country B collapses? What if the U.S. dollar goes up? Or down? These things are happening all the time, yet companies are seldom prepared to cope with them until later.

Include simulations in all training sessions. Encourage your salespeople and in-house staff to suggest scenarios. Don't limit participants to people who know the country. The idea is to encourage everybody to learn about all competitors, all markets.

For many marketing executives, playing "What if?" is a problem. They don't like to think about what could go wrong. They are committed to an upbeat approach to marketing. There's nothing wrong with this, but it does pay to be prepared for an occasional knock. The hypothetical scenarios I have suggested are quite realistic. You probably have already gone through several similar ones in real life, and will do so again.

Try this out at your next training session: Pick out one of your priority markets and ask, "What is the worst thing that could happen to us here?" Once the "worst thing" has been defined, discuss ways to avoid it or to minimize its impact. This is a healthy and productive training exercise. In the process you will uncover new tactics and strategies. You will also be prepared to spare your company much of the embarrassment and grief that comes from being caught with your knickers down.

Simulations don't all have to be based on bad news. Include a good-news situation from time to time. What if Competitor B reduces its sales force by 30 percent? Pulls its field manager out of Latin America? Discontinues its top-of-the-line model? Loses money for a third straight year? A positive simulation can help prepare you to jump in and take advantage of favorable conditions.

Playing "What if?" can be great fun in addition to being useful. Adopt it as a regular game at all sessions.

Esprit de Corps

Training also means creating a company atmosphere that encourages all employees to think of international as a dynamic arm of the company and not as an exclusive club of prima donnas who spend their time sunning themselves in tropical paradises.

Salaried staff who work in the relative tranquility of a 9-to-5 job have no idea what it is like to chase customers in a strange country, to have business meetings at impossible hours, to sit in a grubby airport all night waiting for a delayed flight, to work on a sale for months only to find that the customer never had a budget to start with, to spend a weekend flying from one country to another and ending up with a devastating case of jetlag.

Without the support of the people back home, the morale of overseas field managers and salespeople will suffer. If you haven't launched a serious effort to build up and sustain employee understanding, start one today.

Do it informally; you don't need formal training sessions. Try holding "international evenings" that take advantage of visits by field managers, agents, and VIPs from abroad. Invite spouses and companions, but keep the groups small so everybody can rub elbows. A guest of honor can give a brief, chatty talk on the customs and habits of a foreign country. Avoid speeches, particularly about business. Nothing is more boring than to listen to how great the company is, and to be lectured on market penetration and growth factors. Avoid, also, films or videos unless they are short, fun, and unique. Don't show them just because you can't think of anything else.

These international sessions don't have to be held regularly. Anything that becomes routine loses some of its freshness and appeal. Keep the sessions spontaneous and informal.

Think Global!

"What if?" games can also promote global thinking. A field manager in Bogota may come up with a novel approach to a scenario in Bahrein. This should be part of trying to keep all salespeople in the field posted on what is happening in other markets, what problems are being faced by fellow salespeople and agents.

Don't limit global thinking to your international operation. Extend the concept to domestic sales. Try to do away with the barrier which may now exist between your domestic and international divisions. Both are really part of the same team. You will help create better understanding and mutual support if you bring together small groups of domestic and international salespeople from time to time. Give them hypothetical scenarios to work on. It will prove stimulating, revealing, informative, and unique.

You will uncover hidden sales talents where you least expected to find them. You will strengthen the ranks of your international rapid deployment sales force. You will boost morale on both sides.

Who Does the Training?

You, the international marketing manager, are responsible for training, unless your company is large enough to afford a full-time training manager. Base your approach to training on these three simple rules:

1. Don't train one person when you can train several at the same time. The effort is the same, the effect geometrically greater. (But don't go beyond a dozen trainees at a time.)

2. Avoid sloganeering and bravado. Boastful statements like "We're going to step right into the lion's den!" referring to a tough territory, or "We'll beat the hell out of any competitor, anytime, anywhere!" are silly and unnecessary. They don't teach anything. They are usually spouted by executives who will never have to face the lion in the den!

3. Don't get carried away with your vast storehouse of international savoir faire. Don't hog the podium. Others have something to say: field managers and salespeople; staff from your order-handling, accounting, shipping, promotion, and mailing departments; by all means the intelligence manager.

Bring in marketing consultants, university professors, retired diplomats and military officers, others with specific overseas experiences. They can be useful in making people aware of cultures, manners, dress habits, humor, customs, motivation.

Take advantage of visits by your agents. Don't limit them to thirty-minute sessions in the privacy of your office and then bid them good-bye because you are too busy. Foreign visits are unique opportunities to add to your staff's knowledge of the world. Schedule training sessions around visiting agents. Let them run their own show. They will be tickled. You will make them feel important, part of the company. Do the same with visiting intelligence sources, nakodos, and VIPs.

Education versus Training

Training is about the nuts and bolts of your business, your competitors, your markets, and how to sell. Training is vital, but let's not forget the power of education. If you have any scholars in your company with more than a passing knowledge of world history, culture, and religions and you have not been using them in international marketing, you are overlooking valuable assets.

Like most corporations, yours probably has an increasing number of staff and executives strong in specialized, career-oriented training and weak in history and culture. For most people, these are not the world's most exciting topics. Few individuals (including government leaders) bother to study history, which is one reason why the same mistakes are repeated generation after generation.

A high executive in an international French company told me that until seeing a rerun of the movie *Gone with the Wind* a few months ago, he had assumed that the American Civil War had been fought between the United States and South America. This gap in his knowledge of U.S. history probably did not cost his company calamitous sales losses. But with the United States as the company's top market, knowledge of *some* U.S. history certainly could not have hurt!

You don't need to put your entire staff through exhaustive history courses, but try to use in-house talents, or occasional teachers, to give your people background on at least your priority targets.

New Training Media

Videotapes and videodiscs are an excellent way to extend your training of salespeople and agents. Each medium has a specific purpose. Videotapes are a quick and inexpensive way to demonstrate new products and sales techniques. If you have a tape duplicator, you can run off copies and mail them to field offices and agents.

Another good use of videotape is to bring information from the field to the main office—videos of overseas installations, agents' showrooms and personnel, overseas meetings. This material can be edited and duplicated for the benefit of people in other countries, and used at home to give your in-house staff a "live" look at field situations. If you sell complete installations such as laboratories, clinics, or kitchens, a video of the proposed location can be useful to your technicians back home when they prepare proposals and quotations.

As videocameras become smaller and lighter, encourage your field people and agents to use them often. Make cameras available to them.

There are two problems to watch out for with videotapes:

1. Amateur videos tend to be lengthy, poorly edited, boring. In a large company you can avoid this by assigning a professional video producer to

your international marketing division—someone who can create original videos, edit those produced by others, and train your traveling salespeople on how to shoot their own. In a small company you may find that someone among your employees knows enough about video production to do the same on a part time basis. If not, use an outside service.

2. Most of the world operates on the PAL standard. Videos produced in the United States (NTSC standard) will not work on PAL-system TV videoplayers and monitors. If your traveling salespeople shoot videos with portable equipment for playback back home, this is no problem. If you are sending videos to other countries, you have two choices. One is to produce a PAL version of the same tape; this is expensive and unnecessary. The other is to encourage overseas offices and agents to have players that will handle both systems.

Videodiscs are a revolutionary medium to store and retrieve visual information. The CD-ROM version (Compact Disc, Read Only Memory) is a single disc with as much information as a 3-meter pile of 360K diskettes. A CD-ROM disc can store an encyclopedia of twenty volumes or more, complete with a dictionary, a thesaurus, and an extensive index that lets you search for words in seconds (almost every word is indexed). The cost is less than half what you would pay for the printed and bound version.

CD-ROM discs are durable, measure 4.75 inches (120 millimeters) in diameter, are etched once at the factory then covered with a coating of clear plastic. The coating is transparent and protects the disk from dust. A laser beam "reads" the disk. The beauty of the system is that you can random-access the data and mix audio, color still frames, and motion picture sequences. One disc can store fifteen hours of audio and 15,000 color images, for instance.

Videodiscs are ideal for reference. They cannot be erased. In international marketing you can use them to store visual (still and motion picture) information on products, specifications, schematics, installation instructions and charts, parts lists, answers to technical questions—an enormous storehouse of information which can enhance the effectiveness of salespeople and agents in the field. Portable, compact players will soon be on the market. Every one of your people in the field will be able to carry one.

You can produce videodisc updates every three or four months at less than $50 per copy, from information contained in a computerized master which can be kept current day by day. Compared to the cost of updating, producing, and mailing printed manuals and bulletins, the cost is minimal.

In a large organization, you can produce several videodisc versions from your master. For your salespeople in the field, as well as your RDF, create videodiscs which contain not only product, sales, and technical information, but also basic files on countries, agents, and competitors.

For agents you can emphasize selling techniques, ordering procedures and information, technical problems, suggested advertising layouts, samples of direct-mail promotional pieces, displays at trade fair exhibits, and other information that will not change substantially from month to month but which should always be available for reference.

For important end users and VIPs you can do videodiscs which demonstrate your product and its applications, including scenes of important installations and information about your company and services.

Another important medium in coming years will be two-way teleconferencing. Latest codec technology allows you to transmit audio and video through a single telephone line. A demonstration in your showroom or factory can be easily transmitted to any number of stations around the world, with viewers able to talk back to you and be seen on your own screen.

In international marketing, teleconferencing will open excellent opportunities to organize meetings involving a number of people scattered around the world. The advantage of face-to-face meetings and discussions of marketing problems will add yet another weapon to your arsenal.

Modern technology can revolutionize your training and marketing. There is a serious danger, however. The more people rely on technology, the more lax and careless they may become about their own responsibilities and functions. Don't let your salespeople and agents place excessive reliance on videotapes and videodiscs. Set up a dynamic, interesting, constantly renovated training program, and don't excuse anybody in your international marketing organization from participating.

Training and the Agent

In-house training is as vital to a local agent as it is to an international organization. The same principles apply, projected on a regional or national scale. If you represent a number of international firms, take full advantage of their training, such as seminars and lectures by their field managers and salespeople, also films, videotapes, and videodiscs.

Don't rely entirely on your suppliers, however. Create your own training scripts, based on your own interests and objectives. In addition to your own executives and support staff, try to draw on the expertise of local university professors, embassy commercial officers, and consultants. Find out what courses are available at local business schools, consider the possibility of special training sessions tailor-made for your company.

Give priority to improving the quality of your sales force, your intelligence gathering, your nakodo network, and your support services. These are some of the most important qualities an international supplier looks for in a local agent.

Most agents confine their training to occasionally sending a salesperson or technician to the headquarters of an international supplier. This is an excellent idea, except that this type of training is usually limited to a handful of individuals—invariably deserving ones who are rewarded with a free trip abroad. Less deserving ones, who may need the training desperately, are left behind.

Dovetail your training with the programs offered by your suppliers. Introduce more and better training to your entire organization, and put pressure on suppliers to help you. In fact, you should be reluctant to represent any supplier who is not ready to offer a specific, effective, and continuing training program.

10
"Smoothing"

A special lady from Topeka, of solid pioneer stock, taught me many years ago that "the squeaky wheel gets the oil." Holler loud enough—about a salary raise, a washing machine that doesn't wash, a bank teller who lost your deposit—and sooner or later someone will do something about it, if only to shut you up and get rid of you.

There are squeaky wheels in every company. Ask your shipping department, and you will find that some salespeople never stop hollering until their orders are handled.

The problem with squeakers is that by putting pressure on your staff, they cause somebody else's order or request to be sidetracked and delayed—no way to run a railroad. If you give priority to those who shout the loudest, less aggressive people stand to lose. In the long run your international marketing operation will suffer, because preferential treatment creates jealousies and infighting that eventually can kill the enthusiasm and productivity of your sales force.

If you have squeaky wheels, something is not running the way it should. It's time to overhaul your machinery. You need what my friend Musa Hammad, in Saudi Arabia, calls "smoothing."

Smoothing, says Musa, is putting an order through its stages—from proposal to order confirmation, production scheduling, invoicing, delivery, installation, and settling commissions—without any bumps or squeaks. It means anticipating problems and contingencies, having ready solutions.

Smoothing is up to your support staff. Only when you clearly establish that their role is to provide the logistics your salespeople need to do their jobs can you expect to have a smooth, squeak-free international marketing operation. The task of logistics is to help convert proposals into orders and eventually into money in the bank, as swiftly and as painlessly as possible.

Indispensable Logistics

The support functions without which your international marketing cannot function include intelligence, personnel recruiting and training, promotion, preparation of quotations, mailing, follow-up, invoicing, shipping, accounting, collections, commission payments, communications, and technical support.

Some functions must be totally under the control of international marketing: intelligence, personnel recruiting and training, promotion, quotations, mailing, follow-up. Ideally, international should also have its own technical team and communications system.

Other logistical support is usually run as separate departments serving international and domestic marketing, even in large corporations. It includes order processing, invoicing, shipping, accounting, collections, and commission payments. Foul-ups in any of these departments can create serious problems in international marketing. Unfortunately, in most companies the international marketing manager has little to say about how these services are run. It is not easy for an international marketing manager to seek smoother invoicing procedures when the persons responsible for invoicing also work for a domestic sales manager. To say nothing of the fact that department heads will not take enthusiastically to attempts to deplete them of personnel, or to someone trying to tell them how to do their jobs.

International marketing managers who have to approach support staff outside their control hat in hand to get something done are at a disadvantage. In U.S. firms whose main goal is the domestic market, domestic sales managers squeak the loudest and the most often, and international business often is sidetracked. There is only one person to blame for this: the chief executive officer. Smoothing starts from the top. It is up to the CEO to promote cooperation, teamwork, and understanding.

The situation is worse in conglomerates where support functions may be carried out in offices located in another building or even in another city, by people who are never even seen by international marketing managers, and who therefore never have the slightest contact with overseas sales conditions and problems. Blending these services into a smoothly working machine is a tough job for any CEO. The difficulty is compounded where the services are carried out by another subsidiary in the conglomerate.

There are many reasons why a logistics organization may develop squeaks. My favorite seven are excessive staff, ignorance, lack of coordination, obsolete jobs, boredom, lack of initiative, and nineteenth-century communications.

Trimming the Fat

The U.S. Army has often been criticized for supporting an enormous agglomeration of headquarters and support activities staffed with underemployed clerks and staff officers, while fighting units go undermanned. You can say the same of many companies.

I cannot tell you what constitutes the ideal ratio of field to support personnel. This depends on your product. But the more people you have in logistics in relation to your field force, the greater the danger of losing control, things going wrong, and bureaucracy spreading. Excessive staff inevitably results in redundant and obsolete jobs.

Unless yours is an exceptional company, it is safe to assume that you have too many people in the office and not enough in the field. Start with this premise, and you will have taken your first step toward trimming the fat out of your operation.

You can also assume that within your in-house staff you have enough talents to perform all the functions you need in international marketing, without going outside for help. In other words, trimming the fat is more a matter of *reassigning* people rather than of firing them and hiring replacements.

Your main problem, if you are the international marketing manager, is that the heads of the various logistics departments not under your control will fight any incursions from your side and may also resent suggestions on how to streamline their operations. Once again, this is a job for the CEO. Nobody else can set the tone and promote close teamwork.

We have already discussed the importance of combing through your staff to pick out recruits for your overseas sales force and rapid deployment force. Recruits can come from almost any department.

Next, find people for your intelligence apparatus. You need an international intelligence manager and, if yours is a large company, possibly two or three assistants, researchers, intelligence evaluators, and editors. In a small company at least one person should be involved in full-time intelligence.

Another vital logistics area to be staffed is training. At least one person has to be in charge of training full time.

Intelligence and training personnel should be recruited from among people who have been involved in market research, secretaries and assistants who have had close contact with international operations, personnel who have done some travel abroad, scholars, and linguists.

Reassigning personnel doesn't necessarily mean hiring new people to take over the jobs that have been left open. Put people to work in productive jobs in support of international marketing, eliminate obsolete functions. Here is a unique chance to get rid of a lot of fat without upsetting your staff.

Make a serious assessment of each job and decide if you really need it. Abolish the ones that serve no real purpose, that make no significant contribution to international marketing. Only you can decide which jobs can be abolished, but let me make a suggestion. Many secretarial and assistants' jobs have been created to save executive time. The trouble is that the time saved is used by many executives to go home early, take a longer lunch hour, play golf, or find an excuse for another useless staff meeting.

At home, many executives have no problem handling their computers, manipulating word processing and spreadsheet software, communicating by modem with other computers, and accessing electronic bulletin boards. As soon as they walk into their offices on Monday morning, however, they become so helpless they cannot even dial their own telephones.

Dictating a letter to a stenographer is just about the most archaic function still performed in offices today—with the twenty-first century just around the corner! Look at your office procedures with a critical eye and you will easily spot several other functions still being carried out as they were in the days of sailing ships. They persist because that's the way they have always been done and nobody has ever thought of changing things.

The men and women who today perform outmoded functions could be put to much better use in productive jobs, such as covering foreign embassies, finding in-house intelligence links, keeping track of intelligence sources abroad, helping recruit and train new blood for your RDF.

The Need to Know

If I phone your Chicago headquarters from Abidjan or Amman, you can assume two things: my call is important (at least to me), and I need information. The last thing I want to hear from whoever answers the phone on your side is "Well, I really don't know who would handle that," or "They are all out to lunch and there is nobody here to help you." Or infinite variations on the same theme.

Yet this is precisely what happens all too often. The larger the company, the more ignorant the personnel you deal with, for a simple reason: each person has a narrow, limited view of the company and its functions. There is another, more ominous, reason: most people really don't care. They work on a need-to-know basis. You do your job, I do mine. And never the twain shall meet!

People are hired for specific tasks and are seldom exposed to anything else. A quick tour of a company, a rough idea of the functions of different departments, may be included in a sketchy orientation session. It is seldom enough.

Ignorance is invariably management's fault. Freezing people into jobs perpetuates a cubbyhole mentality that works against the idea of close teamwork. When someone in your office tells a caller from overseas that he or she has nothing to do with whatever you want to know, the only thing that is accomplished is to antagonize a buyer, agent, nakodo, or intelligence source. The ultimate loser is your international division; the ultimate winner is a competitor.

You cannot, obviously, have staff who know everything that goes on in every department. But you can try for a happy medium. Rotate your personnel from time to time. Don't let anybody sit too long at the same job, no matter how good he or she may be at it. Give everybody a taste of different departments.

This is not to say that you should take a highly qualified bookkeeper and shift him or her to run the postage meter in the mailroom. But it could help if the bookkeeper occasionally spent several days actively working on quotations, intelligence gathering, order processing, and even on mailings.

Expose your office staff to a wide range of functions. This is the best way for them to learn what is going on, who does what, and what are some of the typical problems involved. Have them actually *do* things rather than sit and look over somebody's shoulder. In a large corporation, where departments may be rigidly structured, the need for in-house rotation is even more pressing.

A client of mine in West Germany successfully carried the idea of personnel rotation beyond the office, into the international field. The company operates three small sales offices abroad. Whenever a manager, assistant, or secretary takes a vacation, the firm sends in someone from the international head office back home as a replacement for three or four weeks. Everybody gains. The branch office does not have to hunt around for a local temporary replacement who knows nothing about the business. The replacement gets a change of scenery and routine. In fact, the assignment is seen as a coveted bonus. The company benefits from the replacement's new and direct experience in a foreign market. The cost is small: essentially the airline fare.

Try in-house rotation among your departments and send people overseas if you have offices in different countries. If not, try to give them temporary jobs working for agents overseas, particularly if it can be combined with a vacation. You will enlarge your staff's horizons, making them more knowledgeable about what goes on in your international operation. And perhaps the next time I call you from Abidjan or Amman, someone at your end will be reasonably well informed and confident enough to keep me from hanging up and calling a competitor of yours!

Rotation will discourage complacency and routine. It can stimulate initiative and help you discover hidden talents. Perhaps the sharp bookkeeper will take like a fish to water when exposed to order processing, and will come up with smoother procedures.

When Hand and Glove Don't Fit

Another serious problem which arises when people don't know what their neighbor in the next cubbyhole is doing is lack of coordination. Consider this royal foul-up, which happened to an electronics manufacturer—a firm with infinite cubbyholes—on a project in Argentina.

Juan Vasco, the company's agent in Buenos Aires, sends in an encouraging report about a possible big project and asks for catalogs and spec sheets covering the full line. The request lands on the desk of the international marketing manager, who relays it to the "marketing services department," the people whose main job is to send out literature and other support materials. They send Vasco a carton full of catalogs.

Juan spends weeks working on the project. His prospect eventually settles on a model which has all the right features. Juan telexes the manufacturer, specifies the model and quantity needed, and asks for an immediate quotation. The international marketing manager takes a look at the telex and replies:

"Sorry, this model was discontinued ten months ago for lack of sales. We have no plans to replace it."

Juan is flabbergasted. Weeks wasted on a product which no longer exists! How does he face the prospect? What can he offer now? What happened?

Quite simply, nobody in international marketing had bothered to tell marketing services that the model had been discontinued. Catalogs were sent out to Juan Vasco (and to other agents and end users) as a matter of routine. In fact, marketing services was delighted to ship the catalogs. They had a big pile of them stashed in one corner and nobody seemed to want them.

Don't think that this could not happen to you! Lack of coordination is an ever-present danger. It is worse when people don't see each other face to face, and when you assume that everybody else will do their thing efficiently and on time.

I get a strange feeling when visiting firms where everybody works behind closed doors. You walk down long, quiet, empty corridors, not quite believing that hundreds of people are busily performing their chores in tiny offices all around you. You wonder if anybody really knows or cares what happens next door. When people get used to doing specific, narrow tasks, they lose interest in the final result. They become bureaucratized. I remember a discussion once with a department head in a Latin American ministry of education about the dangers of bureaucracy.

"You are putting too much emphasis on the medium, not enough on the message," I insisted.

"There *is* no message!" came the reply. "There is only administration!"

Cubbyholes promote privacy, poor communication, and damage to teamwork. If you are head of the international marketing department of a large organization, some of your staff may not even know when you are away on a trip. The administrative wheels keep turning at their own pace, but the damage to sales can be costly.

A Touch of Spice

Many of the problems which plague international marketing departments (or any other administrative operation) are caused by *boredom*. The problem of Juan Vasco and the outdated catalogs can be caused by boredom. When people are bored, the fault lies with management. You hire people for specific jobs, assign them to a desk, and as soon as they are reasonably well trained they become mere cogs in a machine. How can you make in-house staff work exciting? We have already seen two ways: by trimming the fat and through rotation. A third way is by making a conscious effort to eliminate boring jobs, especially if they are also obsolete. We have already looked at one: taking shorthand dictation.

Obviously you cannot wipe out boring jobs entirely. Every job has an element of boredom. Some, however, are more boring than others. Wherever you find a boring job, try to eliminate it. If not, you and your staff should put your heads together and find ways of dispersing the most insipid and uninteresting functions among a number of people who may at the same time have other, more "exciting" things to do. Being alert to this problem, and trying to do something constructive about it, is in itself a salutary move.

We have seen some of the new, creative, and productive functions you can introduce in your international logistics, such as developing and running an intelligence apparatus and a network of nakodos. Find people on your staff who can be switched to these positions, and you will help reduce boredom and generate initiative.

Take a Letter

You've heard a lot about international direct dialing, communications via modems and satellites, computerized telex machines with amazing memories, access to databanks, electronic bulletin boards, fax machines that transmit entire pages of drawings in seconds, and a lot of other exciting communications and informatics goodies which are just around the corner.

The speed of communications has increased astronomically. The speed of thought—the ability of humans to absorb and use the new technology—has not. Do you still push an intercom buzzer and call your stenographer-secretary to dictate a latter? Or do you swivel around and tap out the message on a computer by your desk?

Poor communications is still a major obstacle to international sales, even in large corporations. Messages can be flashed from the other side of the planet in a few seconds. But from the telex room to your office they may take hours, if not days! Mail delivery has also deteriorated. It takes longer today for a letter to go from Washington to London than it did fifteen years ago. With luck you get one-week delivery. If you still communicate with overseas agents, field managers, and end users by mail, and if it takes you three days to answer a letter, you have a reply time of at least ten days in your correspondence. In today's world, this is ridiculous, especially if on top of the daily routine of marketing and order processing you add an intelligence apparatus and a network of nakodos to your organization.

The smoother and faster your international communications system, the more you will shorten the selling process. Your overseas orders are the end result of a progression of messages between your international office and the field, each hopefully contributing answers and information until the buyer has a clear picture with which to make a decision. You may not be able to speed things up at the other end, but at least try to do all you can from yours.

Here are a few principles on how to speed up international marketing communications.

1. *Answer immediately.* Don't let a message lie on your desk longer than overnight. If possible, answer all telexes the same day. It is inefficient and rude to ignore a telex. At least telex the sender that you are evaluating the message and will have an answer soon.

2. *Stop writing letters, abolish dictation.* Use the telex or the telephone in all international operations, unless the subject is unimportant, or if it involves an agreement which has to be set in writing. It is cheaper to telex a brief, direct message than to dictate a letter to a stenographer and have it go through the transcribing process. A dictating machine is quicker but still involves additional human labor.

3. *Learn how to write.* Get into the habit of concise, no-nonsense writing. This takes special skills. Rambling through a dictated letter is easy. Reducing it to a single paragraph is not. Hire someone to give short, prac-

tical courses to your international staff. It will pay off in smoother, quicker, more productive communications.

4. *Get a telex.*   The telex is nothing new. Yet thousands of firms in the United States still don't have one, not even an old, slow clunker. If you do any international business at all, invest in a telex.

5. *Put in a special international phone line.*   Anybody who calls you from overseas should be able to get directly to your international marketing department, bypassing switchboards and others who have nothing to do with sales abroad. Get a separate number, and save it entirely for incoming international calls.

6. *Accessibility.*   Don't tell an overseas caller that Patricia MacGregor, your international marketing manager, is busy at a meeting and "cannot be disturbed." This is infuriating and insulting. If indeed she is at a crucial meeting (meetings seldom are!), someone else should be readily available to answer calls intelligently. It is a cardinal sin for an international marketing executive to be incommunicado without having made sure a responsible person can answer important overseas calls.

In addition to a telex, install a recording system to take messages during off-hours. When London takes a break for lunch, New York is about to get out of bed and most of California may still be watching a late movie on TV the night before. Saturday and Sunday are working days in most of the Islamic countries. Nobody in Saudi Arabia will expect you to be in your Chicago office on Sunday morning, but make sure their message can be received and recorded, and tell your overseas people that the line and recorder are always open. On the other hand, Thursday afternoons and Fridays are the Islamic weekend, which means that while there is no rush to answer a telex from Saudi Arabia on Wednesday evening or Thursday, you should do it by Friday night so that the person at the other end can act on it first thing Saturday morning—the start of the Islamic week.

Assault by Computer

The computer—in addition to its spectacular potential in intelligence gathering and retrieval, order processing, and all other phases of international marketing—is about to become a powerful tactical weapon for field people as well.

Portable, battery-operated units will give field people an enormous storehouse of ready information while traveling, the ability to communicate swiftly with the home office via telephone lines, and the ability to access new data the same way. Intelligence sources and nakodos armed with portable computers will also multiply their own usefulness many times.

Electronic publishing of manuals, service instructions, product data, sales techniques, promotional materials, and other vital information will inevitably spell the difference between success and failure for many firms in international marketing.

One reason informatics and modern telecommunications are not fully used today in international marketing is ignorance. Many executives remain unconvinced and suspicious. They just don't know what modern technology can do for them.

The answer is to bring in specialists, hire telecommunications and informatics consultants to go over your international marketing operations and show you how to get rid of horse-and-buggy methods which may be costing you a lot of business.

Smoothing and the Local Agent

Constant smoothing at the local level is vital not only to agents but to the international suppliers they represent. Slow or archaic procedures can slow down the flow of presentations, quotations, proposals, orders, and day-to-day communications. The smoothest-running international organization will run into serious snags when a local agent takes six days to answer a telex or forgets to pick up bid documents for a million-dollar project. In the long run it is the agent who suffers through the loss of franchises.

If you are a local agent, ask the suppliers you represent to look at your organization constructively and show you ways to make it run more smoothly so that your procedures dovetail with theirs. Take advantage of this free advice to create a tighter and more effective organization.

PART 3
On the Attack

11

Terrains of Your Choice

The goal of international marketing is to achieve the highest sales volume with the least expenditure of resources. In your global strategy, your choice of targets is therefore critical. If you are a small company, your strategy may focus on ten to fifteen countries, with five of them as priority markets. But even if you are an international giant, you still have to allocate priorities. You cannot apply maximum pressure and resources everywhere.

How many markets or countries you can attack intensively depends on the size and quality of your sales force and your resources. We have discussed the advantage of concentration. Don't water down your resources by spreading them all over the world, or over more countries than you can cover effectively.

You have probably identified priority markets through careful research. You have looked at their total imports, the source of their purchases, import trends over the last five or six years, market shares held by your competitors, local tariff and tax conditions, distribution patterns, and many other things without which you could not reach an intelligent decision. You have assigned regional managers or salespeople to cover these priority markets regularly, and you may even have established your own offices in some of them.

In short, your systematic approach to selecting priority markets was impeccable, along traditional and accepted patterns. The only problem is that your competitors may have done exactly the same thing, so you all end up with similar global strategies, locking horns in the same arenas.

Look at Saudi Arabia in the 1970s. Everybody went there. If you wanted to shake hands with your competitors, all you had to do was check in at the Intercontinental Hotel in Riyadh almost any week in the year except during the hot summer months and the holy month of Ramadhan. The market was booming. Competition was deadly.

I am not suggesting that you ignore major markets. Just as the United States is the prime market for Japanese and European manufacturers, so is Western Europe for U.S. firms. To bypass these markets is inexcusable. The point is, however, that size alone is not the only way to measure markets. If you go for bigness and purchasing power, you will miss many attractive markets.

The prospect of head-on collisions with competitors may stir up the adrenalin in many international marketing executives, but this is not the best way to build up sales and make profits. Wars of attrition can be costly.

Develop, instead, a strategy based on finding markets where your competitors are not yet firmly entrenched and you have a reasonable chance of acquiring field superiority over them.

The search for new markets and priorities is endless. Your intelligence apparatus must be constantly alert to new openings, your rapid deployment sales force ready to assault any market that seems promising. If you have been working with a system of rigid territories, you will have to shift your thinking to a policy of flexibility, mobility, and concentration of power.

You should assume that your competitors have all done their homework just as methodically as you have. Don't underestimate their research and intelligence gathering. Try to stay ahead of them by adopting a strategy that avoids costly clashes. You don't always have to go in through the front door. Look for back doors and open windows!

A Sense of Perspective

We usually think of markets as countries: the French market, the Brazilian market, the Japanese market. An obsession with this concept leads to distortions and an unbalanced application of power. You spend as much time and effort on a country like Qatar (population 200,000) as you do on France (55 million).

Your regional manager responsible for France may stop four or five days in Paris while the regional manager in the Middle East spends the same amount of time in Doha (80,000) and Bahrein (350,000).

European firms seeking to crack the U.S. market instinctively think of New York, Chicago, Boston, Houston, Atlanta, or San Francisco and may never give a thought to St Louis, Kansas City, Jacksonville, or Omaha—all of which are several times the size of many small countries, in population and purchasing power.

In the 1970s hundreds of companies expended enormous resources going after business in Saudi Arabia and the Arabian Gulf, an area with a combined population of less than 12 million. Rich, yes. But there is a limit to how much a country can buy, and what share of the pie you can reasonably expect to get. Larger and more stable markets were ignored.

Break away from the rigid concept of countries as markets, and look instead at realistic targets within them, whether they are states, provinces, municipalities, or even cities. There is more to Brazil than Rio de Janeiro and São Paulo. Put large countries in perspective. Break them down into smaller pieces and then find out how strong or weak the competition is in each of them. If you find and attack three or four soft spots in a large country, eventually a pattern will evolve which will allow you to move into the rest of the market.

Through the Back Door

If your business depends on government orders, there may not be a way to outflank your competition. You may have to ram your way through like everybody else. But if you are after a large, diversified market, dissect it and you may find unexpected ways to get into it.

If France, for instance, is a priority market for you and your top competitors, you and everybody else are sure to head for Paris. But what about Lyon (1.2 million metropolitan area population) and Marseilles (1 million)? Have you ever made a study of these and other major cities in France? Are your competitors represented locally? Are their local agents authorized to buy directly from the factory or do they have to go through a Paris wholesaler or distributor?

The climate in Lyon and Marseilles may be more encouraging than in Paris. Local agents may have seen little of your competitors' regional managers and traveling salespeople. They may be fed up with Paris wholesalers. Trying to crack the French market through Lyon and Marseilles could be a very smart strategy for you.

There's a possible bonus to the back door strategy: a price advantage. The costly effect of the distribution pyramid typical of most large, complex markets can be minimized. If the Lyon and Marseilles agents ordinarily would have purchased from a national wholesaler or importer in Paris, you can now deal directly with them at lower prices, having eliminated a middleman.

The back door approach does not mean trying to find agents in Lyon or Marseilles who can develop sales throughout France. This defeats the purpose of going after immediate, local opportunities. *Try to find strong, qualified, local agents who can crack their immediate markets.* Your concern is to capture Lyon and Marseilles and surrounding areas. The immediate purpose of the back door strategy is to strike where the competition is weak or nonexistent, and to achieve maximum sales concentration through a dominant local agent. Whether or not you can move into the rest of the country is not important. In the process, however, you will acquire a presence and direct experience in the market. Find two or three soft spots in a large country, make the most of whatever price advantage you can gain, and you will have an excellent foundation for an eventual national organization.

Think twice before giving a national franchise to an agent who is not set up to deal with an entire country. The agent, excited with the prospect of getting national exclusivity, will promise you the moon. You, eager to get the territory "settled" so you can move on to the next country, may be tempted to give in. In the end you may kill your chances in the immediate market, and your agent will never be able to compete effectively in the big city. You will ruin a good local agent, and fail to make a dent in the larger, national market. The back-door approach means striking in a terrain where you can dominate your competitors. Don't weaken or dissipate the power of local agents by asking them to do more than they are capable of.

The United States and Canada are notable examples of countries which can be approached through the back door. There are many others. Here are some of them.

West Germany has no real "front door." This is one of the most decentralized countries commercially. You can set up agents in Frankfurt, Duesseldorf, Munich, Hamburg, Cologne, Stuttgart and several other major industrial cities. In all of these cities you will find firms actively involved in the national market. If your competition is soft in Bavaria, get the best agents for Bavaria only, and don't ask them to cover the rest of Germany for you.

In Belgium most companies normally head for Brussels, but you may do better if you start in Antwerp.

In Italy all roads may lead to Rome, the center of government, but Milan is the largest commercial city. You won't find Milan free of competitors. It may be easier to crack Italy through Turin or Genoa.

Spain's traditional center of power has always been Madrid, but Barcelona is just as attractive commercially. Try also Valencia, a city often overlooked by foreign manufacturers and suppliers.

Switzerland can be approached from any number of cities, and you will find local agents who operate strictly in their immediate cantons. Most companies focus on Zurich and Geneva.

Sweden is usually penetrated through Stockholm or Goteborg, seldom through smaller but also important cities such as Malmo, Linkoping, and Nykoping.

The Netherlands, though geographically small, offers many openings other than Amsterdam. Consider Groningen, Breda, Rotterdam, Utrecht, the Hague, Eindhoven, and Apeldoorn.

In the United Kingdom, London draws foreign companies like a magnet, but you have a wide choice of other major cities, among them Birmingham, Manchester, Leeds, Liverpool, Bristol, and Glasgow. As in West Germany, you will find many firms in Britain's leading cities capable of selling throughout the United Kingdom. Try to differentiate between them and those concentrating on their immediate areas, if this is your goal.

Australia is made up of distinct markets centered on Sydney, Melbourne, Adelaide, Brisbane, and Perth. Most national distributors are in Sydney and Melbourne, but not all of them cover distant Perth adequately.

Brazil is a prime example of a market where most companies concentrate on two cities (Rio de Janeiro and São Paulo) and virtually ignore the rest. There are excellent opportunities to explore competitors' soft spots in provincial markets based on Porto Alegre, Curitiba, Florianopolis, Belo Horizonte, Salvador, Recife, Fortaleza, Belem, and Manaus.

Colombia has three main commercial cities: Bogota, Medellin, and Cali. Not all may be covered effectively by your competitors. Take a look also at smaller but still reasonably attractive markets such as Cartagena, Bucaramanga, and Barranquilla.

Venezuela is less diversified, but you can look at Maracaibo as a market distinct from the big capital city of Caracas.

Mexico is more than Mexico City, in spite of the massive concentration of population and industry in its greater metropolitan area. For back-door approaches to soft markets you have many choices, among them Monterrey, Chihuahua, Guadalajara, Durango, Puebla.

Saudi Arabia is another country which can be approached from different places. For government business you need a foothold in the capital of Riyadh. But consider also agents in Jeddah and Dammam if you want to go after these highly developed commercial cities.

One of the smallest decentralized countries is the United Arab Emirates. An agent in Abu Dhabi may be unable to make any headway in Dubai, two hours distant by car, and vice versa. The third largest city is Sharjah. Find out where your competition is concentrating, and try to hit the softest of the three.

South Africa is a decentralized country. Most firms try to establish national distributors based in Johannesburg, occasionally in Cape Town. Several other cities, however, offer opportunities to exploit back-door markets: Durban, Port Elizabeth, Bloemfontein, Pietermaritzburg, and Pretoria, the national capital.

Nigeria is decentralized. Although the country still depends heavily on

Lagos, there are possibilities for back-door markets in Ibadan, Kaduna, Kano, and Enugu.

China, still a difficult but increasingly attractive market, is a conglomeration of provincial and municipal markets which must be approached one by one. You may want to establish a single, exclusive national distributor, but you probably won't find one; distribution facilities in China are still scarce and primitive. There are no national marketing networks.

Most firms try to penetrate China through Beijing, Shanghai, or Guangzhou (Canton). With rare exceptions, whatever arrangements you arrive at in these three cities will have little effect on your business throughout the rest of China. Japanese firms have learned the importance of hitting every major city directly, with their own salespeople.

You will find the field less crowded and more receptive if you go after some of these provincial capitals: Hangzhou, Nanjing, Hefei, Zhengzhou, Jinan, Taiyuan, Xian, Tianjin, Shenyang, Wuhan, Changsha, Nanchang, and Fuzhou.

There are no dealers or distributors in China's provincial capitals. The only way to penetrate these markets is through your own salespeople (provided they are fluent in Mandarin, and hopefully conversant in at least one other Chinese dialect), an aggressive agent based in Hong Kong, or (ideally) both. To cover China you need all the personnel you can get.

India is also widely diversified. To try to cover it through a single national agent could be a mistake. It makes more sense, as in China, to seek local markets. Bombay, Delhi, and Calcutta are the main bases of operation for national distributors. Try, however, to analyze possibilities for hitting local markets through agents in Bangalore, Madras, Hyderabad, Ahmadabad, Kanpur, Bhopal, and Indore. Your competitors may be overlooking some of them completely.

The Front Door or Else

Some countries offer you no back-door choices. You go in like everybody else, through their main commercial cities or capitals. You can try outflanking your competitors and finding provincial soft spots, but the pickings will be slim. The advantage of these markets is that they are highly concentrated; your major prospects are all within a tight radius. The disadvantage is that when business is booming, they are highly competitive. Projects and prospects are very visible.

Here are some of the most centralized markets.

Argentina, with 60 percent of the population clustered around the country's capital and the neighboring province of Buenos Aires, does not give you much choice of back-door markets. Rosario, the second largest city (population about 1 million), is itself in the same province. You may try to open up back door markets in cities such as Cordoba, Santa Fe, Mendoza, and Corrientes. But for all practical purposes Argentina is Greater Buenos Aires (capital and province)—just as Chile is Santiago, Peru is Lima, and Uruguay is Montevideo.

In Turkey the big business center is Istanbul, but all government business is transacted in Ankara. A survey of Greece may encourage you to consider Salonika as a back-door market, but unless you land in Athens you won't have much of a foothold in the country. Egypt is unquestionably a centralized country; the action is all in Cairo.

In Western Europe, some of the more centralized countries are Denmark, Finland, Norway, Austria, and Portugal. In Southeast Asia, you could make a case for a back-door approach to Indonesia, but since most business for foreign firms has to do with government projects, you cannot operate efficiently without a base in Jakarta.

South Korea is entirely centralized. You either set up an agent or a sales office in Seoul, or you stay out of the market. Also centralized are Thailand, Malaysia, and of course Singapore.

Virtually all of Africa, with the exception of Nigeria and South Africa, is made up of centralized countries that for all practical purposes offer no opportunities for back-door markets.

Japan is unique. At first glance you may identify back door markets based on important cities other than Tokyo, Osaka, and Nagoya. Such as Kobe, Sapporo, Fukui, Nagano, Niigata, Hiroshima, Kagoshima, Nagasaki, Kumamoto, and Matsuyama. However, even if you find powerful agents who are strictly local, you will quickly learn that it isn't easy to deal with them due to the rigid structure of the Japanese distribution system. Orders from local dealers to overseas suppliers are channelled through trading companies; the communications problem is virtually insurmountable.

Prime examples of highly centralized countries where opportunities for back door business just don't exist are, of course, the Soviet Union and the East European countries.

The Importance of Minimarkets

In the quest for targets, global strategies often overlook lucrative minimarkets. The usual procedure is to draw up a list of countries by imports of your particular product, and concentrate on the biggest ones at the top of the list. That is a sensible approach, but how about taking a look also at some of those at the bottom of the list—or at countries which don't even appear in international trade statistics because their purchases have been too small to make the list?

Why bother with a Tonga (100,000 population) when a prize plum like Australia is another couple of hours' flight to the west?

It isn't a question of giving up a big market in favor of a little one. If you have not included minimarkets in your global strategy, chances are that neither have your competitors. There are valid reasons why you should not forget the Tongas of the world.

In a minimarket ignored by the competition, you may capture an overwhelming share of the business. This could net you a larger profit than you might get from a market ten times the size but extremely costly and competitive, where all you can hope for is a 10 percent share.

In a minimarket you are closer to end users. Marketing and distribution patterns are less structured. You deal directly with local agents or end users, bypassing intermediary wholesalers and importers. You either end up with a bigger profit per sale, or you pass on the extra margin to local agents. You also get to know VIPs personally. Seeing people is easier than in a big, busy country; government bureaucracy is less overwhelming. You are more visible.

Business opportunities and projects in minimarkets will attract less worldwide attention in the industry. While every one of your fifteen competitors is fighting tooth and nail for a project in Indonesia, you may be in the driver's seat in a much smaller one in the Solomon Islands.

To decide which minimarkets to include in your strategy, you will have to mobilize your intelligence network. Be particularly alert to major projects financed by the World Bank, the Asian Development Bank, the African Development Bank, and bilateral aid. A country with a low standard of living may be hopeless as a consumer market, but this in itself may create the need for a multimillion-dollar development project. Check the development loans being approved for some of the small nations of Africa, the Caribbean, Asia, and the Pacific. You will be surprised at how substantial they are, and how much procurement they generate.

Here is a list of some minimarkets—population 1 million or less.

In Africa, one of the most prosperous countries is Gabon (population 750,000), thanks to its abundant natural resources. Other small countries worth noting, all of them recipients of international and bilateral loans, are Botswana (900,000), Cape Verde (350,000), Comoros (360,000), Gambia (700,000), Guinea-Bissau (850,000), São Tomé and Principe (200,000), and Swaziland (600,000).

In the Indian Ocean, international and bilateral assistance is financing projects in Mauritius (1,000,000), Seychelles (90,000), and the Maldives (175,000).

In the affluent Arabian Gulf, these small countries have attracted considerable competition in the last ten years: Bahrein (425,000), Oman (900,000), and Qatar (220,000).

One of the richest (per-capita) countries in the world is Brunei (240,000) in Southeast Asia.

Many Pacific island nations have become independent, among them Fiji (650,000), Kiribati (70,000), Solomon Islands (240,000), Tonga (100,000), Vanuatu (125,000), and Western Samoa (160,000).

Independence has also come to many islands in the Caribbean region: Antigua (80,000), Bahamas (250,000), Barbados (260,000), Belize (150,000), Bermuda (75,000), Dominica (100,000), Grenada (120,000), and St. Lucia (140,000).

Europe's best-known minimarkets are Luxembourg (370,000), and Monaco (30,000). Less known, in fact usually ignored, is Iceland (240,000), a sophisticated country with a high standard of living and purchasing power. Other small European nations worth noting are Cyprus (650,000) and Malta (350,000).

Between the minis and the maxis are many medium-size countries often overlooked in global strategies. If you draw a list of those with populations between 1 and 8 million, you will come up with attractive markets such as Austria, Switzerland, Denmark, Hong Kong, Finland, Norway, Israel, New Zealand, Ireland, and Singapore,

Why Not Some Tough Markets?

Your global strategy should include a serious evaluation of markets that are difficult to crack. Some may be dominated by competitors. Others are tough for political reasons. Don't be too quick to write them off. The more difficult a market, the more it will discourage your competitors. It may pay you to find out if you can cope with its problems and quietly carve out a niche of your own.

For U.S. firms, these are difficult or closed markets (as of May 1986): Iran, Libya, Cuba, Kampuchea, Vietnam, North Korea, Nicaragua, the Soviet Union, Poland, East Germany, Czechoslovakia, Hungary, Bulgaria, and Rumania. International marketing executives are not always sure how to handle them, and often the easiest way out is to ignore these markets without even taking the trouble to check government policy toward them.

What do you really know about these tough markets? Have you ever evaluated them? How does your competition—domestic or foreign—deal with them?

Six of these countries are closed to U.S. exporters. Cuba, Kampuchea, North Korea, and Vietnam have been declared "embargo destinations" by the U.S. government. Libya and Nicaragua are also out of bounds, under the emergency powers of the President of the United States.

There is no U.S. embargo against Iran, only restrictions on products intended for military use and crime control. Sales to the USSR and East European countries may be subject to export licensing by the U.S. Department of Commerce; this generally refers to high technology and applies usually to other countries as well.

While none of these markets is going to be handed over to you on a platter, it pays to examine them seriously for their immediate potential and for long-range strategic planning. Leave politics aside and try to learn which of them could be a favorable market for your product. Play "What if?" What if Cuba, Nicaragua, Libya, and Vietnam opened up? Stranger things have happened. Twenty years ago nobody ever went to Saudi Arabia. Ten years ago would you have imagined that one day soon thousands of eager salespeople would be stumbling over each other in Beijing and Shanghai? When Saudi Arabia and China suddenly became "in" markets, were you ready to go after them intelligently or did you have to suffer a long, costly, and painful learn-as-you-go experience with everybody else?

The world keeps evolving; things never stay the same. Cuba may never open up in this century. Or it could open next year.

It will not take much effort or resources to develop intelligence on today's closed markets. Study them one by one. Check U.S. government regulations, you may find a way in through a crack none of your competitors ever noticed. What is more important, however, is that you will gain valuable insight on how to attack these markets if some day they should open up.

In the USSR, the East European countries, and Iran, opportunities are more realistic. These markets are not officially out of bounds to U.S. firms. Find out if your product is a type which needs export licensing to each of these countries, and under which conditions. There are no blanket rules for the USSR and the East European countries. Licenses, when required, are handled case by case.

A few comments on trade embargoes.

Embargoes seldom, if ever, cause governments to crumble or change their policies.

Embargoes favor your foreign competitors. One person's embargo is another one's good fortune. British and West German firms (along with firms throughout the rest of Europe, Japan, Canada, and most other exporting countries) continued to do business with Libya long after Washington imposed an embargo on U.S. exports to that country.

Trade-oriented countries as a rule don't mix state with trade policies. Cuba, again, is a good example. Even Spain, while still under the rightist regime of Francisco Franco, was doing business with Havana. When the U.S. government imposes an embargo, it sends a signal to smart international marketing managers elsewhere around the world that here is one more market free of U.S. competitors. It is also a signal to U.S. firms to investigate exactly what the embargo means in terms of their products.

How tough and tight is an embargo? Are you allowed shipments through a third country? From subsidiaries or joint ventures? Can U.S. citizens travel to the embargoed country, or will you have to use other sales contacts? Check current regulations with the nearest district office of the U.S. Department of Commerce.

Behind Protective Walls

Some countries are tough for economic reasons. Brazil and India, for instance, are highly protective of their industries. You cannot ship personal computers to Brazil because of widespread local production. If tariff and import licensing requirements are so restrictive that you don't stand a chance to penetrate the market with your line, what else do you offer which could be salable in the particular country, assuming the market is worth the effort?

If you are a manufacturer, you can probably sell subassemblies, plant machinery and installation, technological know-how, or technical services. If your target is Brazil, typical buyers of these products and services will be Brazilian manufacturers, or firms interested in setting up licensing or joint ventures with you. Or you may want to establish your own subsidiary.

All of these avenues are worth exploring if the potential in Brazil is attractive. What do you expect to get out of Brazil? If you promote local manufacturing, how will this affect your sales elsewhere in the world? Will you be able to produce inexpensive versions of your product in Brazil, which could then be fed into your international marketing network? What share of the Brazilian market will you be able to capture? How will Brazilian manufacture help you fight competition, in Brazil and elsewhere?

These questions all highlight one key point: When you evaluate a tough, protected, but potentially attractive country like Brazil, plan long-range. The prospect of a multimillion-dollar turnkey project may be exciting, but if this is a one-shot deal in which you deliver a plant, get paid and walk away, all you will accomplish in the long run is to create a new competitor. Although the Brazilian firm's initial target may be Brazil, sooner or later it will become ambitious and start scouting for world markets of its own.

This has happened all too often in the last forty years, particularly in Japan, to the regret of many U.S. firms.

The answer is to get a piece of the action. Try to control the operation in the target country, either through a joint venture or a subsidiary of your own, which can then sublicense local manufacturers. Negotiate agreements which will involve you in marketing, including worldwide distribution rights.

Your two goals in setting up such an operation are:

1. To capture a good share of the local market
2. To help boost your overall global sales

You can accomplish both if you pick the right countries. Among the newly industrialized ones to consider in your global strategy are Argentina, Brazil, Mexico, Turkey, Pakistan, India, and China. If you establish manufacturing in any of these countries, you may be able to open up markets around the world which had been closed to your products for political, commercial, or economic reasons. This will give you a more flexible global strategy, perhaps even a parallel international marketing organization under your overall control, with its own human and promotional resources.

The Developing Nations Market

The volume of development loans to Third World nations from organizations like the World Bank is rising. The World Bank's annual lending volume is expected to exceed $20 billion annually by 1990 (compared to $11 billion in 1985). Most of this money will be used to purchase goods and services from the United States, Canada, Western Europe, Japan, and other industrialized nations.

Expect substantial increases also in the budgets of all the other organizations involved in international financing.

Internationally financed projects are highly competitive. They attract bidders from all over the world. However, few of them bother to cultivate project directors in the recipient countries personally, particularly if the country is small, extremely poor, and out of the way.

Evaluate Third World projects; include them as part of your global strategy. Here is a situation where you can put some of the people in your rapid-deployment force to good use, by sending them out for personal calls on project directors in countries not regularly covered by your field managers and salespeople.

While substantial financing will continue to be approved for major countries such as Argentina, Brazil, Indonesia, Mexico, and Nigeria, don't overlook projects for many of the small sub-Saharan nations, all of which will be included in new projects.

Global Reminders

History repeats itself—so do errors in international marketing. As you pick out markets, including small and tough ones, remember that the object of international marketing is to develop the highest volume of sales with the least expenditure of resources. Exactly how much? Do you have a specific, realistic global target? What are you looking for in dollars? How does each market fit into the overall picture? Are you ignoring markets which would require less effort and produce more sales than some of the ones you are now fighting for? These are only some of the questions you should answer as you set down your global strategy.

Remember also that following the same path as the competition does not really give you much of an edge over anybody. You become part of the pack. Trying to break into countries that have already been worked over by the competition—stepping into the lion's den, so to speak—may only wear down and exhaust your resources, for minimal returns.

When Markets Go Bad

It is just as important to find and penetrate new markets as to know when to pull out of one which has not lived up to your expectations. Set up realistic objectives, and give yourself enough time to achieve them. If at the end of the day you seem to be making no real progress toward your goal, consider pulling out. You can always keep the market on the back burner and have it covered by a diplomat.

When should you pull out? Only you can tell how long it takes to cultivate buyers for your product. International marketing depends on patience and perseverance. You cannot rush the process. Give a country at least three or four years.

Make sure, before beating a retreat, that you have used your resources to the full. If you didn't make it in a market because you didn't deploy enough salespeople, you may be abandoning an attractive market to your competition. Be alert, also, to political and economic shifts, particularly a violent change of government.

The bottom line is profits; territories are secondary. Develop your sales where opportunities are best, use your resources where they will do you the most good. Don't sacrifice manpower for the sake of maintaining an ineffective operation in a country which is going stale.

Local Terrain and the Agent

Agents who operate in narrow national territories may think they don't have much flexibility in their choice of terrain. This is not true. Even in a minimarket an agent should be able to identify market levels or areas where the competition is weakest, if only by picking out best-selling products and dropping unsalable ones.

For instance, if you are an importer of household furniture and carpeting in Abu Dhabi and a supplier tries to sell you a wide range of products for your showroom, you should be able to narrow down your selection to those items for which there is a reasonable local demand. To carry items which might sit in your showroom for months is a waste for you and the supplier. You will both be better off if you put all of your resources into selling the most productive items.

In a large, decentralized country, such as Brazil, Colombia, Saudi Arabia, or Australia, look for soft, back-door regions which international suppliers may have neglected, and point them out to the firms you represent. They will welcome your creative approach to the local market—a fresh departure from agents who depend entirely on suppliers to tell them where and how to promote a product.

12
Aggressive Leadership

Your success in international marketing depends on concentrating authority under a single, strong, unmistakable central command whose main tasks are to:

1. Develop short- and long-term strategy
2. Recruit, train, and lead a hard-hitting sales force
3. Mount the strongest possible attack on target markets
4. Supervise a well-oiled logistics team

The buck stops with the international marketing manager. Any dilution of his or her authority will weaken your sales force. On the other hand, too much central command can put a damper on local initiative. When your sales force begins to turn to central command for day-to-day, routine, tactical decisions, and you don't do anything to encourage local solutions, you will start losing some of your muscle.

How deeply central command should be involved in tactical field decisions depends on the size of your operation. If yours is a large one, with offices in many countries and a large sales force covering most of the world, you must delegate authority to local and regional sales managers. If yours is an international operation with four or five traveling field managers or salespeople, direct contact between them and your central command is of course easier. One advantage of this closeness is that central command can maintain a realistic understanding of what is happening in the field, and respond with constructive advice.

When Central Command
Is Weakened

Central command is diluted when it is divided among several executives with the same level of responsibility, such as when a company's marketing department is organized by product groups. Here is an extreme case.

Kolby & Cousins, Inc., markets three separate but related product lines in the United States through distinct domestic marketing divisions. International marketing is handled by three managers operating independently of one another, except that logistics services are shared. Their job is to set up agents throughout the world. They report to the company's president, who theoretically is in charge of coordinating their efforts, defining strategy, and organizing staff support, but who seldom has time for international and knows next to nothing about world markets. There really is no coordination. The managers are jealous of their one-person divisions, seldom communicate with one another, do nothing to help promote one another's products. Essentially they are glorified office clerks with no power of decision.

This situation is not unique; it exists in far too many companies. Kolby & Cousins should appoint one of the three managers as the sole international marketing manager, and put the other two on the road selling the combined product line.

At the other extreme is a conglomerate with a highly centralized international marketing operation for its companies. The producing companies have no involvement in international marketing, there is minimal communication between them and the salespeople in the field. A case can be made for this type of unified international operation when no company in the group was seriously and professionally involved in seeking foreign markets prior to its acquisition by the conglomerate. But to dismantle company-level international marketing departments for the sake of streamlining administration can be dangerous. The conglomerate's central command becomes an intermediary bureaucratic level seldom able to respond quickly to market demands and opportunities.

Strategic Handicaps

To be effective, international marketing must always be positive and aggressive and not rigidly bound by company policies. Rules will lead you into a rut, because they are incompatible with the concept of creativity. No market is a walkover; expect obstacles and problems everywhere. But if things are not going well in one or more markets, your sales force could be laboring under serious handicaps beyond the normal pressures of markets and competition.

The most devastating handicap is to ask your sales force to sell the unsalable—when your product just doesn't stand a chance. A product can be unsalable for any number of reasons: price, color, shape, size, features. Sometimes the problem is easy to solve. You adapt your line to market requirements, you drop the unsalable model and concentrate on others that are easier to move, or you shift to a different sector of the market, one where your competitors may be at a disadvantage.

Sometimes, however, handicaps are not easy to overcome and you face no-win situations which can have a bad effect on your entire operation. One of the worst is when your production line has become too costly to run. Competition from countries with more automated production or lower labor costs can freeze you out of many lucrative markets. This is a problem for many firms in the United States, West Germany, and other high-wage countries in Western Europe. There are three ways you can try to counter this threat.

1. Find favorable markets where you can emphasize quality and features, and where you have cultivated a fairly loyal following.

2. Concentrate on markets where you can eliminate wholesalers and perhaps retailers, and sell directly through your own sales force, giving end users the benefit of lower prices without sacrificing your profit.

3. Slash your production and overhead to the bone, without sacrificing your sales efforts.

None of these options can be long-lasting. They will gain you time while you develop new strategies and product solutions, but all you will be doing is defending a factory which has become uneconomical. Concentrating on a few favorable markets and cutting down intermediaries are positive, aggressive steps. But slashing costs, including the cost of valuable marketing resources such as personnel and promotion, can deplete your resources. Sooner or later you will be squeezed out of most markets.

A better solution is to buy similar products from low-cost manufacturers in other countries and use them to expand your international operations aggressively in as many markets as possible. You may be able to recapture markets you had lost to cheaper competitors.

Finding cheaper sources in low-cost countries is what increasing numbers of U.S. and European firms have been doing in recent years. The temptation, however, is to tack on an excessive markup on the low-cost product, to help defray the losses of your uneconomical production line. Again, you are defending a losing facility. The inflated overhead will minimize price advantages, weakening the impact of the lower-priced product. You can also take it for granted that some of your competitors will also be resorting to similar low-wage sources.

In the school science laboratory industry the problem of costly production versus low-cost sourcing is very real. Company A is committed to maintaining a high-quality but expensive factory producing a line of instruments which have become increasingly unsalable. Company B has abandoned all of its own production and taken on the role of worldwide marketer, offering hundreds of science items through a catalog as thick as the Manhattan phone book. Products are purchased in bulk quantities from suppliers in Japan, Korea, Taiwan, Singapore, and India.

Your company can try any number of solutions to the problem of an uneconomical, possibly obsolete, production line. Including selling it as a package deal to a developing country! As the international marketing manager, your advice will be extremely valuable, although the final decision will not be up to you. Your responsibility is to produce international sales and profits, not to protect an uneconomical factory or try to ram unsalable products into impossible markets.

My own experience with a severe strategic handicap goes back to the case of the Swedish manufacturer of office machines described in an earlier chapter. This was a classical case of trying to ram the wrong product into the wrong market.

Company A, the manufacturer of high-priced scientific instruments, is still doing well in six carefully selected markets while trying to hold on to other markets, but this is a losing battle. The Swedish office machine firm continued to do well in Europe and Latin America with its two-row calculator keyboard, after its serious reverses in the U.S. market. But this, too, was a losing battle. Eventually, on the verge of being squeezed out of most markets around the world, the company successfully overhauled its global strategy in response to market pressures and needs.

There is nothing wrong with concentrating on a few key markets. Somewhere in the world there is a ready market for the same product you are successfully selling in your domestic market. If yours is a small or medium-size operation, to go after six or seven good markets may be enough. But whether you are large or small, the worst thing you can do to your international sales force is to pitch it against insurmountable odds. You will wear down your salespeople, killing their morale and enthusiasm.

If the odds are against you, pull out! Don't waste your sales talents. If you think that some time in the future you may want to go back, put these losing markets on hold temporarily; assign them to a diplomat or to an occasional traveler able to keep up with contacts and agents.

Pulling out of an impossible market is in itself a positive step toward better use of your human and other resources in more lucrative areas. However, make sure you carefully dissect and understand the handicaps that drove you out of the market. If they were caused purely by market conditions and policies, such as protected local industry, impossible import licensing requirements or tariffs, lack of budgets, or no demand for your type of product, there is little you can do about them. You may still have a very salable product, given the right conditions.

But if handicaps are the result of price, the lack of salable features, poor marketing tactics, or better and more aggressive marketing efforts by your competition, a serious reappraisal is in order. You may find easier, more receptive markets elsewhere, but in the long run this is not a healthy situation. Sooner or later the bad news is bound to catch up with you, and if you have done nothing to develop positive strategies you will be in serious trouble.

Learn from your strategic handicaps, but try to avoid them at all costs. Never ask a marketing manager to fight defensive battles. Your international operation must be positive, aggressive, and *always on the offensive.*

Strategy Decisions

Not all of the executives usually involved in strategy decisions are well informed about international marketing. However, a marketing offensive aimed at key targets will not succeed unless all executives stand behind it. You need complete understanding and support from all departments. It is up to intelligence to keep top executives constantly briefed on markets, opportunities, and the competition, through short and to-the-point reports.

How many executives should be involved in determining strategy? The fewer the better. If all strategy is referred to a group of fifteen people, it may take days or weeks to reach decisions. An "international strategy board" may sound like the right approach, but it can quickly become another bureaucratic stumbling block.

A more practical and flexible solution is *not* to organize a definitive group, but to bring people together only when and as needed. For instance, if a strategy discussion will deal with whether or not to produce a 220-volt version of your SWISH-9876 stomach pump, the meeting should include executives with specific knowledge of production costs and scheduling—along with the international marketing manager—but not necessarily the person in charge of promotion.

Meetings should not take place regularly. Keep them down to a few, and as far apart as possible. One of the toughest things to do in a company is to limit the topics to be taken up at meetings. The list can be endless, the waste in executive-hours unbelievable. Don't call an international strategy meeting unless there is something specific and important to discuss.

Legitimate topics for a high-level meeting should include a discussion of new overseas targets and opportunities, major moves by the competition and how to counter them, product salability, new product ideas, political developments and their effect on your current markets, serious strategic handicaps, pulling out of hopeless markets, human resources needs, expanding the field sales force, new offices abroad.

Strategy should also take into consideration the cost of moving into a new market and its relation to expected sales. If resources are limited, a choice of targets will have to be made. Should you target China, a potentially huge but costly market to get into? Or a diversified selection of minimarkets in the Pacific?

Since your sales results will depend on what products you sell and how diversified and adaptable your line is to overseas market needs, a vital question for strategy meetings is what to do about seeking low-cost sources to complement your own line. Consider piggybacking—taking on noncompeting products from smaller manufacturers who are not prepared to go international on their own. Can you market piggyback products without tacking on exorbitant markups and pricing yourself out of the market?

You should also discuss pricing, always vital in international marketing. Ideally, the international marketing manager should have authority to set prices in response to specific market situations, rather than stick to a rigid international formula. This authority can be spelled out in terms of a specific price range.

Strategy meetings should not get into details of case-by-case, market-by-market pricing problems. Everybody will have something to say, not always enlightening, and you will end by wasting dozens of executive-hours. This is a tactical, operational matter for the international marketing manager to decide.

In pricing, as in many other marketing issues, the international marketing manager must be allowed to stand on his or her own decisions somewhere down the line. This strengthens his or her position and the effectiveness of central command.

Field Operations

These are the most important operational functions of central command:

1. Know at all times what is happening in the field, the whereabouts of field managers and salespeople, which major projects are pending, and how they are being followed up.

2. Constantly evaluate market opportunities and needs, and decide what resources are available to exploit them to the hilt. This involves continuous monitoring of individual markets.

3. Maintain close communications with the field. Don't sit back and wait for reports from your traveling salespeople to trickle in haphazardly or until several days after they have returned from overseas trips. Talk to them frequently by phone or telex. This will stimulate aggressive teamwork and give you an opportunity to suggest new tactics, provided you don't

squash their initiative. An international marketing manager satisfied with the lackadaisical pace of occasional written reports (usually too long, incomplete, repetitive, poorly written, and boring) quickly becomes a passive spectator.

4. Consult frequently with the intelligence manager: ask for briefings on the latest incoming intelligence; discuss new information needs.

5. Coordinate all the weapons available in your arsenal: field managers, salespeople, agents, nakodos.

6. Direct and control the rapid-deployment force—where to use it, for how long, and when to recall it.

Does your international marketing manager have the power to carry out all of these functions without resorting to higher executives or staff meetings? In operational situations, every delay in reaching a decision gives your competition more time to take the deal away from you.

Hints on Tactics

Once global strategy is established, the choice of which tactics to apply in each target market must be up to you, the international marketing manager. Your type of product will determine the range of choices available to you.

The ultimate goal is to make the most profit out of each country or territory. Let's review some important points to bear in mind:

1. *Rely on a sound, down-to-earth business approach; establish a reliable sales organization in each market.* Don't go in on the basis of high-level personal contacts and connections, for instance. You can easily get burned.

In the busy years after the oil crisis of the early 1970s, dozens of firms plunged into the Saudi market with their eyes closed, hopelessly misled by promises of agents claiming royal family connections (there are more than 4000 princes in Saudi Arabia!). Most of these connections were useless, most of the so-called agents had no sound business basis with which to build systematic sales.

2. *Pick out the easiest and softest sectors of a market.* Look at your line critically. Which product stands the best chance? Don't feel pressured to sell your entire range. Just because Irene Luscombe, your salesperson in Hong Kong, is going great guns with your model Z-78L does not mean you should demand the same results in Mexico City or Cairo. Remember the bottom line: sales and profits. Concentrate on whatever sells best.

Geographically, look for soft regions—provinces or cities—where the competition is weak, even if this means bypassing the more obvious large cities. As we discussed earlier, your ability to find soft spots can give you a decisive edge over your competition.

3. *Concentrate your sales forces in the most favorable markets, bringing in reinforcements from other areas or from your rapid-deployment force.* Concentrate your promotional resources, also. Invest in trade fairs, advertising, direct mail, and whatever other media suit your product, in the countries where you are likely to get the highest returns. If your budget is limited, avoid expensive international trade fairs and invest instead in promotion schemes in markets where you are strong. The key criterion is your ability to follow up on leads.

Avoid strict promotional budgets by territories or countries. It is silly to run out of advertising funds in a country where business is hot, and to end the year with a surplus somewhere else. Use your resources to the hilt where they can pay off best

4. *Don't apply the same formula everywhere.* Be flexible: adapt to local needs, opportunities, and conditions.

5. *In addition to actively seeking business, your salespeople must be reminded constantly of the importance of winning good agents and nakodos away from the competition.*

6. *Be ready to recall and reassign salespeople.* You may have to do this either because their immediate area has gone into a slump or because the salespeople are needed where opportunities may be better.

7. *If piggybacking is part of your strategy, there are two ways to go:* You can choose unique products with immediate potential. Or you can gauge the needs of individual markets and then try to find piggyback products to meet them. Avoid global marketing commitments unless you know the product is truly salable worldwide. As in many other phases of international marketing, be specific and stay flexible.

Price as a Weapon

Nobody questions the impact of price as a marketing weapon. What is harder to get across is the need for flexibility in international pricing, instead of basing prices on formulas which actually reflect domestic market conditions.

The standard pricing procedure among most U.S. firms is to add a markup that covers domestic promotion, the cost of running branch offices and salespeople within the country, dealer advertising allowances, and many other factors which have nothing to do with overseas sales. Some also tack on an export handling charge, the effect of which is to make the product even more expensive abroad.

If you are "defending" an uneconomical plant, as we discussed earlier in this chapter, your cost accountants have probably worked out an excessive overhead factor which is automatically applied to *any* product sold by your firm, including those purchased from outside, low-cost sources. If the purpose of the markup is to make up for the deficiencies of your own production line rather than to conquer markets, you may be creating impossible odds for your sales force.

Look at international pricing realistically and forget your domestic formulas. Is price a critical factor in penetrating Singapore or Saudi Arabia or Italy? What promotional, distribution, and sales costs will you actually have in each country? What marketing structure? How deep is the distribution pyramid, and what discounts apply at each level? What is the going rate on sales commissions?

The key question: Should your pricing be flexible, reflecting local market needs? Or should you apply a uniform international schedule of retail and wholesale prices and commissions?

The immediate reaction of most companies is to standardize. But this can be unrealistic, and it may keep you from being competitive in some markets. For instance, in the United Kingdom or West Germany, you may need a pyramid of local dealers, wholesalers, and importers. In a small market such as Singapore the importer may sell directly to end users. A salesperson may normally get 20 percent in Sweden but 5 percent in Indonesia. In addition to discount structures and commissions, there are a number of other variables, such as newspaper advertising, direct mail, trade shows, travel, entertainment.

The answer, if you really want to be flexible and react to local market needs, is to develop a price which reflects the real costs of doing business in each market. Your ex-factory cost should not include any overhead or other add-ons and reserves that relate strictly to domestic sales.

The ex-factory price, on the other hand, should include your profit, a reasonable overhead to cover your international marketing operation, promotion, international sales meetings, advertising and service allowances to overseas agents and branch offices, and any other costs which can be clearly identified as strictly international. These add-on costs will not be the same from country to country. Work out a formula for each. You may gain a tactical edge.

To the ex-factory international cost you obviously have to add freight and insurance, giving you a CIF country of destination price. What you should *not* add is a fee for "special handling." This is unfair to your overseas buyer. It will take extra paperwork to handle some overseas transactions, but then, your domestic business is not all clean and paperless either.

Arriving at a cost factor for each country should not be a major problem, if you computerize the proper formula for each one and keep it updated.

A big obstacle to a realistic international pricing formula is the traditional rivalry between accountants and marketing people. It makes no sense because everybody should be on the same side, but internal politics and jealousies are real and detrimental to effective marketing. Accountants are seldom asked to play a positive role in a marketing operation, while marketing field people are not always qualified to make rational cost analyses.

Cost accountants must base their pricing on known factors. Since they are seldom involved in any international activities, they end up falling back on domestic conditions, which they know best of all. Expose your cost accountants to overseas conditions rather than having them rely on reports from field managers and overseas agents. Let your cost specialists see for themselves what market conditions are really like. They can make a valuable contribution to your country-by-country tactics. An occasional trip by a cost accountant to an overseas market, particularly a trouble spot, may reveal effective ways to slash costs.

A realistic pricing policy for each overseas market also involves monitoring exchange rates closely, and reacting to them positively. Reaction to exchange rates is invariably one-sided. If the U.S. dollar goes down in relation to foreign currencies, the usual reaction of a U.S. manufacturer is to increase prices to make more money. But if the dollar goes up and U.S. products become more expensive to a foreign importer, the same manufacturer will seldom think of reducing prices in order to hold on to markets.

While it is logical and businesslike to squeeze every possible drop of profit out of your international operation, to raise prices simply because the dollar is cheaper is not always wise. You may end up with a higher profit per sale, but if you had not changed your price you might have increased your unit sales and captured a bigger share of the market at the expense of a competitor.

Holding on to a market by dropping your prices when the dollar goes up—if you are a U.S. supplier—is not profitable in the short run, but if the market is important it will eventually pay off. You will be smart to hang on, even if your profit is cut to the bone. Find ways to slash some of your operational costs, but don't sacrifice your sales effort. What goes up must come down! Look at the ups and downs of the U.S. dollar in the last ten years! You can expect the same seesaw effect to go on.

Administrative Responsibility

To avoid falling into the bureaucratic pit, the international marketing manager must work hard at keeping things uncomplicated. This is not as easy as you may think. The urge to organize is hard to overcome. Here is an example:

When Rayolex, Inc., decides to go international, never having made the slightest effort to develop international business, the first thing its newly appointed international marketing manager, Donald Glasgow, sets out to do is to "get organized." Thanks to a generous budget, he hires field managers for Latin America, the Middle East, and Southeast Asia, although no serious intelligence has been gathered on any of these markets. Next he hires secretaries for each of them, a promotional manager, a special projects manager, an assistant marketing manager, and half a dozen clerical personnel. The entire group is housed in airy, modern, extensive, and expensive quarters, complete with brand-new desks, the latest electronic-memory typewriters, and a $50,000 computer with individual terminals on each desk (for order processing, filing, accounting, data storage, mailings).

There is only one problem: no business. While the department is getting organized, nobody is out beating the bushes for orders. Everybody is busy organizing and planning. It is like when a writer keeps sharpening pencils, rearranging notebooks, changing the ribbon on the typewriter, and finding sundry other excuses to delay the time when the painful process of writing must begin.

By the time Glasgow and his team are ready to swing into action, his department's overhead has already become a burden and will have to be figured into prices. Rayolex is going international with at least two major handicaps: an established bureaucracy and exaggerated prices. The purpose of the entire operation has been lost. But the company is "organized." There is no message, only administration!

Zarko Enterprises goes about it differently. No fancy offices, no personnel, no computers, just an aggressive international marketing manager who will start off as a one-person sales force, with a factotum and an old electric typewriter at the office. Zarko moves into the international marketplace lean, hungry, and ready to do battle. Procedures will be developed as business expands, constant evaluation of opportunities and needs will dictate how many additional salespeople to hire and where to deploy them. For Zarko there is no administration, only a simple, clear message: Sell!

The lesson is straightforward: Sell first, organize later!

Here is another useful lesson: Don't hire anybody, don't buy anything, until and unless strictly needed.

A Sense of Urgency

Over the years, I have noted that whenever a firm was aggressively and successfully going after overseas markets, there was a certain excitement in the air in its international marketing headquarters—a sense of urgency. Invariably the tone was set by the international marketing manager's personality and style. A slow-moving, methodic bureaucrat will produce a slow-moving, methodic bureaucracy. A busy, active individual, not tremendously concerned with how neat his or her desk may look, is likely to generate vibrations throughout the international division.

Every sales organization needs a measure of hoopla, even if you sell sophisticated computers for scientists and your sales force is made up entirely of highly trained technicians, and not a line of vacuum cleaners sold by sales artists well versed in the techniques of impulse buying. The personal touch makes the difference.

The closer you are to the action, the more dynamic your management must be. In a small operation with a handful of traveling salespeople, the sense of urgency has to be maintained by the international marketing manager. In a large operation where field forces perhaps are controlled by regional or local branch managers, the international manager can afford to be less of a cheerleader. In either situation, however, an enthusiastic approach is vital. Here are some ways to achieve it:

1. *Develop a positive, can-do attitude.*   Don't be too quick to turn down a deal because it is unusual or because of the many things that could go wrong. Get your entire department used to the idea of always "trying to find a way." Remember the case of Sirocco and Frangologia in Chapter 1, and how they reacted to unique business opportunities in Turkey and Inner Mongolia.

2. *Don't ever allow anything to become totally and completely organized.*   I always suspect any office where there are no papers in sight, every pencil is kept sharpened, and I am told that "we are in the process of getting organized." If you have time to keep everything neat and proper, you may be neglecting sales, business is slow, or you have too many people on your staff.

3. *Every order has to generate some excitement.*   You don't need to break out noise-makers and funny hats, but if the order is more than day-to-day routine business, make sure everybody feels good about it. You can achieve this if you have tried to make everybody in your international marketing department part of "the team," and avoided drawing barriers that separate the "in" people from "the peasants."

4. *Don't be overly concerned with the clock.*   Leaving the office on time is human and sensible, particularly if you have to catch the 5.23 at Grand

Central. But an international operation where at five o'clock, day in and day out, there is a wild stampede for the elevators gives the impression that nothing exciting is going on, and that nobody gives a damn. Obviously you don't create excitement merely by making people stay an extra ten minutes. It must come from your ability to instill a sense of urgency and teamwork in your people.

5. *Keep staff meetings short, and don't force people to attend them when they have something more important to do.*   Winston Churchill used to say that one reason for the air of tension in the House of Commons was that there aren't enough seats for all the members. Take a clue from Churchill Never mind if some people at your staff meetings have to sit on the floor or on the arm of a chair. Make sure the chairs are hard, turn down the heat or open the windows, *never* serve donuts or sandwiches. In short, don't do anything to attract more people than are needed at a meeting, or to keep them hanging around long after the meeting has served its purpose.

6. *Avoid small, closed offices.*   Let people work out in the open, where they can see one another. You cannot develop enthusiasm and teamwork when people have nothing to see but computer screens, wall calendars, and the inside of a closed door.

7. *Try to get everybody involved!*   A sense of urgency does not mean a chaotic, sloppy operation with everybody on tranquilizers and antacid pills. It simply means keeping everybody focused on the top goal of international marketing: Selling as much as possible with the least expenditure of resources. There is more to it than simply administration!

13
The Task Force Approach

We have looked at the various weapons in your marketing arsenal: sales-people, a rapid-deployment force, agents, intelligence sources, nakodos, and logistics. How are you using them? Haphazardly, as do most companies involved in international marketing? Or as a well-coordinated striking force?

Superficial research may have reminded you that it is about time you set up marketing in Scandinavia. The territory has been neglected except for the occasional trip of a high-level executive, or sporadic correspondence with firms that have indicated an interest in becoming your agents.

You assign Irene Ivarson to the territory. Her objective is to establish agents and do her best. There are no real targets. She goes through your Scandinavian files, picks up some background information (most of it hopelessly outdated), starts writing and telexing agents, and eventually plans her first trip through the area. Essentially, her assignment is a solo operation, with minimal support from the home office.

What's wrong with this approach?

1. You are looking at Scandinavia as a "territory." The area is actually made up of five countries: Denmark, Finland, Iceland, Norway, and Sweden. Which one is the softest? Where is your competition active or inactive? Are there any ignored back-door markets?

2. You have no clear, realistic goals. You are sending Irene Ivarson to do a job, but there is nothing specific for her to aim at. What do you want to accomplish in Scandinavia? How many people will you really need to do the job? Will Irene be enough? Should you send in some temporary people from your rapid-deployment force? Or is the area big enough for Irene? Could you be wasting her efforts in a market which may be much smaller than you think?

3. There is no coordination between sales and the other weapons in

your marketing arsenal. Has your intelligence fed you current data on local market conditions other than statistics and trade reports? Have there been any nakodo contacts in the area? What do you know about marketing and import conditions in each of the five countries?

4. Your preparation has been poor. You tell Irene to go through old files, you ask her to drop in for a chat, which merely confirms that nobody at headquarters really knows much about Scandinavia. She is starting from scratch and virtually blind. It is as bad as dropping a platoon of paratroopers into strange territory, with sketchy information, old maps, and no idea whether the enemy has one company or three regiments in the field.

Your adventure into Scandinavia is disjointed, follows no plan. It may be typical of how you—and many other companies—dip into new overseas markets. You go into a territory because it is open, it looks good, and it is there. The same is true when you add countries to somebody's territory. Your field manager in Southeast Asia is doing a good job, so you add India and Pakistan to his or her bailiwick perhaps not only because they look good, but also as a reward. You don't even bother to find out what it will take to capture a decent share of the Indian and Pakistani markets.

The ill-prepared, ill-directed, ill-supported international salesperson is a common problem.

Another common mistake is to sign up for a major international trade fair without carefullly evaluating the market. A trade fair is only one of many marketing weapons, certainly not the most important. In the last few years everybody has been "discovering" China. Trade fairs in its major cities have attracted European and U.S. exhibitors who had never before set foot in the country. Glowing reports about this "awakening giant" have been drawing hordes of executives who are quick to approve a $25,000 investment in a fair but reluctant to pay someone $1000 for an honest opinion on the market. The same happened in Saudi Arabia fifteen years ago, and will happen again somewhere else tomorrow.

Before you sign up for any trade fair, find out first what the market is all about. Is there a real opportunity for your product? Do you have the personnel and resources to do what it takes? If you exhibit in Beijing or Shanghai, for instance, how will you handle inquiries? Who will follow up? Who will stay behind to keep your promotional efforts from losing momentum?

Attempts to alert companies to the perils of flying by the seat of their pants are not always well received. I have on several occasions advised companies to stay away from an international trade fair when I honestly felt their investment would be wasted, only to find that their minds were already made up and all they wanted was someone to eagerly agree with them, not the bearer of bad news!

There is only one way to prepare professionally for market penetration or expansion: Adopt the *task force concept*. Bring all your marketing weapons into a neat, well-coordinated package and go after your markets with the precision of a sharpshooter.

The task force concept involves assembling a team of people in your organization who can make a positive contribution to your attack on a specific target, and benefiting from their combined knowledge.

Don't be in a hurry to send a field manager out on a job. Two more months of careful and systematic preparation will make Irene Ivarson a far more effective saleswoman than if she had boarded the first flight to Copenhagen three days after being assigned Scandinavia.

What You Need to Do the Job

Once your intelligence has identified an enticing target, take the time to look for its soft spots. When you are sure you have pinpointed specific targets, make a serious appraisal of what you need to do the job.

How big is the area? How often should it be covered by a salesperson? How long should each visit last? How many days a year of a salesperson's time will it take to cover the target thoroughly and effectively?

These questions cannot be answered without live intelligence from sources and advisors in the target market. The assessment may take weeks, but it will be worth the effort.

Once you have a reasonably clear picture of what it will take to get into the market, figure out what sales forces you have available to do the job.

Suppose you have decided to go into China. If you have a field manager based in Hong Kong or Singapore, your immediate and least troublesome reaction may be merely to assign China to him or her. The field manager is happy with the added responsibility and prestige, and you settle back happy in the knowledge that someone else is now "in charge" of doing something about China.

Again, no planning. The field manager will have to find a way to squeeze in occasional forays into China while trying to keep things going in Southeast Asia. Something's got to give!

Crazy? Unbusinesslike? Yes, but it happens to be the traditional, unproductive, wasteful approach of many companies.

Had you done a systematic intelligence analysis of China, you might have learned that in order to really do a bit more than scratch the surface you will need a rock-bottom minimum of 100 working days a year of a salesperson's presence in China, just to begin to cover Beijing, Shanghai, and the three provincial capitals identified by your intelligence. This is about twenty weeks, or about four weeks a year for each of these cities.

Does your field manager in Southeast Asia have enough spare time to set aside for this new territory? If so, something is seriously wrong with your marketing strategies and planning. More than likely, however, your field manager may be fully occupied in Southeast Asia. Adding China to his or her responsibilities will seriously weaken you in Thailand, Singapore, Hong Kong, Malaysia, and Indonesia. Your choices are to send in reinforcements to keep up the pressure in Southeast Asia, assign new salespersons (most likely from your rapid-deployment force) to China, or both.

The sales forces available to attack a priority market include field managers and salespeople already in the field, possibly in an adjoining territory, and your rapid-deployment force. Eventually you will appoint local agents or set up a full-time sales office of your own. But in the beginning, when you are trying to establish a beachhead, you must use your own resources from outside the country.

We have already discussed the advantage of concentrating your salespeople and rapid-deployment force, no matter how small in numbers. If you don't have enough people to devote 100 working days a year to China, decide what resources you have and apply them where they can do you the most good in China. If the best you can do is thirty working days a year, focus on one or two provincial capitals, don't attempt to cover the entire country. Concentrate! Cut the market down to your size. Do the best you can with your available personnel, *but do it well.*

In addition to personnel, you have to assess the market in terms of what it will take in other resources. How much will it cost to do the job, in travel, entertainment, local promotion, translations, other expenses?

Your assessment of needed resources must be made strictly in terms of the market itself, without reference to neighboring areas. When you estimate personnel needs, however, you obviously have to consider what immediate resources may be available in the vicinity, and how much *additional* power you will need to do the job.

In a minimarket you may have to look at the potential in an entire region. It could be extremely costly to launch a marketing effort in Vanuatu alone and ignore other Pacific nations, particularly in terms of time and travel.

The Tactical Planning
Task Force

The task force concept can be applied to any number of situations. In international marketing there are three main and vital applications: tactical planning, strategic assessments, and intensive market attack.

For each major market, assemble a task force to put together a clear tactical plan. In most cases it will be made up of the same people: the international marketing manager, the intelligence manager, support staff involved in promotional schemes such as trade fairs and advertising, and someone from cost accounting.

You may need other specialists. For instance, if you are going after difficult markets—Iran, Cuba, Vietnam, North Korea, the Soviet Union, or the East European countries—include specialists familiar with government export regulations, import controls in the target countries, third-country approaches, and other problems. The same goes for protective countries such as Brazil and India.

If production, product design, or specifications are a factor in the market, someone from engineering, R&D, or production should be involved in the task force. It is not necessary to include field managers in the task force. The task force will develop a plan, the field manager will execute it. In fact, delay assigning any salespeople to the target market until you have a clear plan of action. This may sound unorthodox, but it is a good way to look at a market objectively. You really will not know who to assign to a target market—or how many salespeople—until your task force has come up with a realistic plan.

Postpone, also, any major promotions, particularly trade fairs. Don't go into one until you are ready for the market.

When enough intelligence on the target market has been gathered, along with the latest readiness status of your human and other resources, your task force is ready to start creating a tight, well-integrated plan which defines:

1. Specific sectors of the market to be hit the hardest—cities, provinces, and end user categories including government, industry, institutions, and consumers—depending on your product. The targets must be realistic in terms of your resources. Remember to concentrate your marketing power!

2. Which products or models to push the hardest, which ones to soft-pedal or ignore.

3. Desirable goals for the first two or three years, such as number of agents to appoint, sales volume, or market share. Use these goals as yardsticks, not as rigid quotas with which to rap the knuckles of salespeople.

4. Role and penetration of the market by your major competitors, including names and location of agents, leading products, prices, marketing approach.

5. Number of salespeople to be assigned to hit the targets—how many assigned permanently to the market, how many temporarily seconded from your rapid-deployment force, specific tasks and goals.

6. Whether the target can be covered effectively by a field manager already in the general area without sacrificing other sales.

7. Minimum number of working days or weeks to be devoted to the target in the first and second years.

8. Cost of executing the plan, including travel, entertainment, promotion, and everything else tied directly to the market.

9. Cities or provinces where agents should be established (from scratch or additional ones); general qualifications, goals, responsibilities, field of operation.

10. Promotional schemes to be used—media advertising, direct mail, exhibits, seminars—and a reasonable promotional budget.

11. How to coordinate nakodos with existing or new agents, including an assessment of nakodos already in touch with you.

12. Additional types of intelligence sources needed and where to look for them.

13. Special training requirements for the salespeople who will be sent to cover the target, and for support and other staff back home. The task force should have access to your in-house talent bank to find people with whatever unique skills the market may call for.

The task force should be small. Bring in the specialists you need, but try not to have more than five people on the team. Set up assignments and tentative deadlines, encourage task force members to work in twos and threes. Don't rush them, but don't let the exercise drag on forever. No matter how thorough your intelligence, there will be many unanswered questions. If you have a mini-thinktank in the market, put questions to it. Use the phone and the telex as much as possible rather than waste time with lengthy letter exchanges. The longer you delay preparing a plan of action, the more time you give your competition to become more firmly entrenched or to discover a soft spot it may have overlooked. Two or three months should be enough to draw up a realistic plan.

If the market is important enough, let one or two members of the task force take a trip to the country and see conditions for themselves, particularly the cost and pricing specialist and you, the international marketing manager. It should also be valuable to send your intelligence manager to make sure of your existing sources and mini-thinktanks, and to set up whatever new ones may be needed.

Set up a special task force for each market. Members don't always have to be the same. In fact, if yours is a large international operation, try to assign different people to different task forces. This gives everybody an opportunity to be involved in planning, and to learn about field conditions. Work on the task force assignment need not take up its members' full time. They should still be able to carry out their regular duties. Some members of the task force do not have to come from the international marketing department—cost and price specialists, for instance. The task force concept is an excellent way to create team spirit and enthusiasm, and to give your staff a sense of accomplishment.

The final plan drawn up by the task force should be concise and specific so that it can be quickly read and digested. If it runs to more than, say, twenty-five pages, summarize it and attach notes. But try to avoid length; keep your reports trim and lean!

The task force should stay together until the plan is submitted, field managers or salespeople have been selected to go after the market and thoroughly briefed. At this point the task force can be disbanded, and the job of keeping up with the market turned over to the intelligence and marketing managers. Limiting the lifetime of a task force prevents it from deteriorating into another bureaucratic institution, and helps cultivate the sense of urgency, action, and achievement which is indispensable to a well-run international marketing operation.

Task force plans should be geared strictly to specific targets. What works in one country may not work elsewhere. What is important is to maintain flexibility and to encourage all task forces to be innovative. If assignment to task forces is rotated so that no two teams are ever exactly the same, you will achieve an excellent cross-fertilization of ideas and views.

The Strategic Assessment Task Force

Creating long-range strategy is another vital application of the task force concept. Although the business of gathering and evaluating market data falls on the shoulders of the intelligence manager, good planning must blend intelligence with an appraisal of the company's actual resources. A diversified team of four or five people from time to time should take a fresh look at specific existing markets—active as well as dormant ones—and at the company's entire global marketing. This is the best way to keep you from falling into a rut.

If a long-range task force sees opportunities in new markets, or new approaches to existing ones, it should draw up a detailed and realistic plan spelling out objectives and how to achieve them. An immediate offshoot of long-range plans is to help you assess the additional human and other resources you may need to achieve future marketing goals.

A long-range task force can draw a lot of information and ideas from training simulations—the "What if?" games we discussed earlier. It should operate on the same basis as market-oriented task forces: short meetings, occasional field trips, teamwork, and a limited lifespan.

The Attack Task Force

The task force concept is a prime marketing weapon when a market is ripe for sales reinforcements. Put together a team of salespeople made up of regulars already assigned to the territory and personnel from your rapid-deployment force. Consider also specialists in advertising, trade fairs, technical seminars, and other support activities, depending on your analysis of conditions and needs in the particular market.

The field task force must be strong enough to achieve its objectives and small enough to be easily maneuvered. Its assignment should be brief—a few months at most—so that it can generate and sustain an atmosphere of crisis and alertness.

Here is a typical task force scenario. You are a U.S. supplier of hospital equipment. Your intelligence and field managers report a bright outlook for your line in Brazil in the next two years. Major health projects are about to be funded and launched, opening the door to millions of dollars of sophisticated equipment not produced in the country.

Normally one of your field managers stops in Rio de Janeiro and São Paulo every two or three months. Your competition does the same. Now you decide to hit the Brazilian market for two solid months, not only with the field manager assigned to the area but also with two people from your rapid-deployment force and well-trained local sales teams from your São Paulo and Rio agents. You have estimated that in two months your task force should be able to reach directly most of the top end users in the country.

Working closely with your agents, you develop a plan of attack involving demonstrations and presentations in as many hospitals and clinics as possible, interviews with Ministry of Health officials, seminars with doctors and medical professors. You bring in an important end user from the United States for ten days of lectures. You and your agents contact the media, arrange publicity releases, make documentary videos available to TV stations and medical societies. You meet with nakodos and urge them to make personal efforts to stir up all the VIPs they may know. Your intelligence manager meets with existing sources and looks for new ones to fill in any gaps in your information-gathering organization.

Sometime during the two-month offensive you send one of your company's top executives on a brief diplomatic visit, which you hope will include interviews with the Minister of Health, the heads of the largest hospitals, the directors of major health projects, and to give your agents in Rio and São Paulo a boost.

Your two-month campaign is launched, your task force soon builds up momentum and a sense of urgency. Everybody is so excited and optimistic that by the end of the third week you feel tempted to extend the task force's assignment beyond two months.

Don't do it!

A definitive cutoff date puts pressure on your task force to finish its assignments on time. This in turn contributes to a general enthusiasm which is bound to have an impact on end users and decision makers. If you keep things loose, with the possibility of everybody hanging on another two or three weeks—or indefinitely—the task force will lose its punch.

As the two-month offensive moves along, make a realistic evaluation of what resources and personnel you and your agents will need to follow up on all leads and proposals after the task force has left. Work out a plan in coordination with your agents. Make them feel a vital part of the team.

The size, composition, and life of an attack task force depends, of course, on your resources—particularly your budget. If you can't do what it takes to hit all areas of Brazil, then concentrate on a soft region. But no matter how large or small your objective, go to it with full power. A substantial share of the cost of the two-month offensive—particularly local advertising and publicity releases—should be absorbed by your agents. How much, will depend on their territories and whether or not they are exclusive.

Task Force Imperatives

The task force concept embodies all of the major principles we have discussed throughout this book, and which constitute the essence of creative international marketing. To be fully effective, a task force—tactical, strategic, or attack—must be:

1. Lean

2. Directed to a specific objective

3. Flexible

4. Short-lived

5. Innovative

Field Initiative

Your intelligence gathering, recruiting, training, search for nakodos, and choice of key target markets can be hopelessly diluted if you insist on controlling every move made by your field managers and salespeople. Having firmed up a plan of attack, allow your field force enough flexibility of action, encourage innovation.

The desire to keep a tight rein on salespeople is often expressed through petty rules, the sort of thing that comes out of detailed procedures manuals, such as making salespeople fill out and mail reports every Friday afternoon even when there is nothing to report.

Recently, in the offices of a French firm with sales offices in North Africa and the Middle East, I heard this exchange between the managing director and the firm's creative, market-oriented export manager:

"You must set up controls for Amman and Algiers," the director said. "They should be more closely directed from here."

"Why?" the export manager retorted. "Let's leave them alone. They are both doing a terrific job and making a lot of money for us."

"They are not sticking to our administrative procedures," the director insisted. "We must have proper reporting methods."

This minor but irritating duel goes on daily in many companies, forcing the international marketing manager into the role of a diplomat who must constantly achieve some sort of harmony between bureaucratic, deskbound top management and the more volatile individuals who make up the field force. A marketing manager who easily succumbs to high-level administrative dictates is not likely to have what it takes to create a hard-hitting sales force in which individual initiative is allowed full play.

Drawing the line between central command and tactical initiative is not always easy. You must learn to tell the difference between strategy and day-to-day field skirmishes. A well-trained, enthusiastic, and self-confident salesperson should have enough latitude to negotiate prices within a reasonable range, submit quotations and proposals without having to telex the home office, for instance.

A field manager should also have flexibility to deal with nakodos—giving them the green light on specific projects, making commission commitments within reason—and with intelligence sources. While the final decision on appointing agents may be up to the central office, the advice of your salespeople should be given priority.

One sure way to stifle initiative and enthusiasm is to be continuously critical of suggestions from the field. This is a bad habit of international marketing managers who are afraid of making mistakes and therefore prefer to proceed with excessive caution. How often do you say no to a field manager? Here is a hypothetical situation:

You are the marketing manager of a manufacturer of microfilm processing equipment. Your field manager in the Middle East has just walked in with a telex from a completely unknown individual in the United Arab Emirates requesting a quotation for seventeen of your machines; a possible $350,000 deal. You have no agents in the UAE. Your field manager has been too busy in Saudi Arabia, Kuwait, and Egypt, has seldom had time for more than a quick one-day visit to Abu Dhabi or Dubai every year, but is eager to pursue the inquiry. How are you *inclined* to react? Will you be upbeat and excited about it? Will you let the field manager go ahead and see where the inquiry may lead? Or will you start thinking about all the things that could go wrong even if the inquiry is legitimate? For instance, you have no service in the UAE. What if something went wrong with the machines? What if there are no competent local technicians? What if . . .

More often than not, I have seen these sorts of deals turned down by supercautious international marketing managers! If you are inclined to be suspicious and negative, you will rapidly stifle the initiative of your sales force. If you are by nature an optimist, you will probably always try to find a way before giving up on a possible deal. This approach will help you develop an enthusiastic sales force.

In most firms, the secret is to encourage field managers to think as if they worked for a small firm, regardless of how vast your organization may be. Not all of them will necessarily jump at the chance. At any level of responsibility, it is always easier and safer to avoid making waves.

Field people may be reluctant to display creativity and initiative for fear of risking their jobs. This is not unusual, even among top executives. The answer is to build up the right attitude within your organization, through training and by example, so that everybody understands the value of new ideas even at the risk of occasional mistakes. Getting your field managers involved in strategic planning and training sessions is one way to achieve this attitude.

Some field people may not be sufficiently imaginative to come up with new ideas, or they may be too timid to assume responsibility for local decisions. This is a problem for those in charge of recruiting and training. Simulations and other training sessions in which specific scenarios are discussed openly can stimulate a person's thinking. Reluctance to make decisions can be overcome if you, the international marketing manager, try to turn as many tactical problems and situations as possible back to the salesperson and make him or her come up with an answer.

Initiative and the Task Force

The task force concept goes hand in glove with initiative—whether the task force is made up of executives and support staff, or of field sales people. Cultivate initiative throughout your entire international marketing operation—among your own field and branch managers, salespeople, agents, intelligence sources, mini-thinktanks, and nakodos. Start with yourself!

14
Jump-off

No book can ever claim to be a comprehensive guide to creative international marketing. All it can to is tickle your imagination and get you started on gaining a sharp edge over your competition by breaking away from ordinary patterns.

Use your imagination and be flexible!

Go over the concepts we have analyzed in this book, bend them, change them, twist them to fit your needs, add some of your own, throw out those that don't fit. And when you finally come up with a plan, don't freeze it. Be ready to change it to meet market conditions.

The first hurdles you will run into will be within your own company. Cynics, skeptics, procrastinators, and timid souls will not take readily to a marketing philosophy that calls for a bit of guts and derring-do. You will find them among executives who will balk at approving unorthodox marketing procedures, and among employees who are reluctant to become involved.

In short, don't look for overnight converts!

Even field managers and salespeople may not take readily to creative marketing schemes, preferring to stick to the true-and-tried methods they have grown accustomed to. Never mind. You don't need to convince everybody at once. Find out which people in the field and on your support staff are likely to welcome innovation, and begin with them. A gradual start will give you a chance to experiment with different ideas and find out which ones work best for your company.

If yours is a small and young international operation, with only a handful of people covering key markets around the world, you have a unique opportunity to become creative before you become entrenched in rigid company policies.

The things we have discussed in this book—effective intelligence gathering, nakodos, a swift and mobile sales force, modern communications and informatics, flexibility in choosing terrains, the task force concept—are not revolutionary discoveries. The secret is to tie them together into a potent marketing package and to make the package work for you.

The fast pace of modern communications and the need for quick reactions to changing market situations will make the international marketplace increasingly tougher, even hopeless, for firms that continue to operate as they did just a few years ago. The more bureaucratic your firm, the quicker it could fall prey to lean, hungry, and more aggressive newcomers.

Market conditions can change too fast for firms that rely on traditional methods. A sharp drop in the price of oil, the rise of a major international currency, trade embargoes, the political opening of markets which had been shut off from the rest of the world—these are only some of the developments which can, virtually overnight, play havoc with your neat policies and strategies. A quick and intelligent reaction to these changes can help you cut down your losses when things go sour, or take advantage of new opportunities.

In the next ten years which "difficult" or closed countries will open up? Which of today's bullish markets will wither away? What role will be played by export-oriented firms in newly industrialized countries? Which countries are likely to contribute to your biggest overseas sales and profits? There are no answers. There is an urgent need to develop intelligence, to create long-range strategies, and to be prepared.

To get into a vast and complex market like China, frequently mentioned in this book, you will be better off with unorthodox game plans than with traditional techniques. There is nothing about China that will quite match your experience in other markets and areas. But finding new markets requires not only being constantly alert to new territories, but also improving your position where you have already gained a foothold. Remember not to be misled by territorial assignments and responsibilities.

Perhaps one of the most crucial suggestions made in this book is the importance of finding out what it really takes, in human and other resources, to get a decent share of a market. What counts is not how many countries you are trying to penetrate, but how well and how thoroughly you go after them. Better a sustained, intensive, well-planned attack on six markets than a half-baked, slow-paced campaign in twelve.

The fear of making mistakes can also be a major stumbling block. Many companies were burned in the Middle East during the petroboom. They rushed into the area without any preparation, did nothing to develop an effective intelligence service, signed up agents who claimed magic connections with the royal family, ignored the need for systematic, day-to-day salesmanship and professionalism.

However, refraining from taking action in order to avoid repeating the same mistakes will not get you anywhere. Most of the executives and sales people who committed blunders in Saudi Arabia and other Arab markets in the 1970s will never claim responsibility for them. The finger is always pointed elsewhere—at the government, an agent, an unreliable nakodo. If you want to benefit from your mistakes, admit to them, dissect them meticulously, find out where you went wrong, and make sure you don't repeat them.

A word about agents. Unless you set up your own branch offices, you cannot have an effective international operation without them—importers, wholesalers, distributors, retailers, whatever type of local enterprise it takes to move your particular line. Agents are part of the traditional marketing pattern.

Although I have focused in this book on the need for new, creative marketing approaches, the agent remains a vital element in any international operation. Work closely with your agents, develop your marketing schemes in cooperation with them. Everything we have discussed in this book, including the importance and role of the nakodo, will work best when there is close and effective teamwork between you and your agents. Encourage them to be original and innovative. Make them an integral part of your intelligence and marketing organization, include them in your training schemes, discuss with them soft back-door markets in their territories, urge them to train their own rapid-deployment forces and coordinate them with yours.

Although the concepts of creative international marketing are not unique, not all of your competitors will have adopted them as a well-integrated weapon. History is full of cases when people were shown the way but refused to follow. However, don't let this lull you into complacency. The worst thing you can do is lightly and disdainfully dismiss your competition as a minor nuisance. Train your entire staff—in the field and in support jobs—to respect your competitors and to expect every one of their salespeople to be superstars in the field. This is the only way to keep your people on their toes, well prepared, well honed, on constant alert, and battle-ready.

Creativity in international marketing is inevitable. Ignore it and you won't last. Adopt it and you will gain a tactical advantage over many of your competitors. Put *them* on the defensive.

Take your first step, no matter how small.

Start today.

Review of Principles and Concepts Appearing in This Book

- Marketing battles are won or lost by men and women.

- Modern communications make it too easy to pass the buck.

- The four main weapons of creative international marketing are market intelligence, human resources, productive logistics, and flexible game plans.

- Intelligence is enhanced when you emphasize the importance of people rather than of countries and companies.

- Shadow the competition's most talented marketing executives and salespeople.

- Nobody should go on an overseas trip without a shopping list of desirable intelligence.

- Don't underestimate intelligence which does not come from executives or international marketing people.

- Intelligence is wasted when you don't debrief employees and executives who have been abroad.

- Intelligence sources should get the facts, be specific and brief, and report quickly.

- Nobody should do something for nothing; you have no control over a source which works for nothing.

- The bigger your intelligence files, the more quickly you will forget what is in them.

- Keep your intelligence databank entries brief, constantly cut and edit.
- Your striking power depends on numbers, quality, mobility, concentration, clear objectives, and global teamwork.
- Put as many active salespeople "on the line" as you can afford.
- Fixed territories imply a dispersal of sales forces.
- In many international marketing situations a better job can be done by people whose prime talents are *not* selling.
- There may be a worldwide demand for your product, but the reasons people buy it are not always the same.
- Don't be eager to introduce yourself.
- Ask, listen, and learn; don't rush to talk business.
- Hotel rooms are not soundproof.
- Don't train one person when you can train several at the same time.
- Trimming the fat within your support staff is more a matter of reassigning people than firing them.
- Freezing people into jobs perpetuates a cubbyhole mentality.
- Cubbyholes promote poor communications, poor teamwork.
- The speed of communications has increased astronomically; the speed of human thought has not.
- In the quest for targets, don't overlook minimarkets and tough markets.
- It is just as important to penetrate new markets as to know when to pull out of one which has not lived up to your expectations.
- Don't bind your international marketing by rigid policies; rules will lead you into a rut—they are incompatible with the concept of creativity.
- Never ask a marketing manager to fight defensive battles.
- Pick out the easiest and softest sectors of a market.
- Concentrate your sales forces where they can do you the most good; bring in reinforcements from other areas or from your rapid-deployment force.
- Don't apply the same formula everywhere. Be flexible, adapt to local needs, opportunities, and conditions.
- Keep trying to win good agents and nakodos away from the competition.
- Be quick to recall and reassign salespeople when their immediate area has gone into a slump or because they are needed where opportunities are better.

- Develop in each overseas market a price which reflects the real costs of doing business there.
- Sell first, organize later!
- Don't hire anybody, don't buy anything, until and unless strictly needed.
- Don't ever allow anything to become totally and completely organized.
- Every order has to generate some excitement.
- Adopt the task force concept.
- A task force must be lean, directed toward a specific objective, flexible, short-lived, and innovative.

Appendix **B**

Useful Addresses

U.S. Department of Commerce (DOC)

The export-service arm of DOC is the International Trade Administration (ITA). ITA's Foreign Commercial Service maintains offices in 120 foreign cities in 63 countries considered "principal trade partners of the United States." Among the functions of overseas offices are gathering data on export opportunities and country trends and identifying and evaluating local importers, agents, distributors, and other business organizations.

Business leads dug up by the ITA's Foreign Commercial Service are published in *The Commerce Business Daily*. This includes trade leads as well as information on foreign government procurement notices.

Another useful DOC publication is *Business America*, a biweekly. It carries articles and statistics on foreign trade developments, markets, and trends, and regularly lists all upcoming promotions abroad sponsored by the U.S. government. Annual subscription is $57.

To subscribe to either publication, contact the Superintendent of Documents, U.S. Government Printing Office, Washington, DC 20402, telephone (202) 783-3238.

In Washington, ITA maintains an Export Counseling Center worth contacting; call (202) 377-3181.

ITA offers a number of useful services. An Automated Information Transfer System links small computers in ITA district offices in the United States, with forty-three overseas posts, making market information accessible worldwide. The system creates computer files of U.S. exporters and foreign importers and tries to match them.

TOP Bulletin, a weekly publication, lists all trade leads received by ITA in the preceding week from all countries. The information is now available on computer tape.

An Agent Distributor Service helps you identify foreign agents, and will provide you a report of up to six possible candidates.

World Traders Data Reports give background information on individual foreign firms.

178

To subscribe to these services, contact the nearest ITA District Office or write Client Service, Trade Information Services, U.S. Department of Commerce, P.O. Box 14207, Washington, DC 20044.

District Offices

Albuquerque, NM 87102, 517 Gold SW, Room 4303, (505) 766-2386

Anchorage, AK 99513, P.O. Box 32, 701 C St., (907) 271-5041

Atlanta, GA 30309, Suite 600, 1365 Peachtree St., N.E., (404) 881-7000

Baltimore, MD 21202, 415 U.S. Customhouse, Gay and Lombard Sts., (301) 962-3560

Birmingham, AL 35203, 2015 2nd Ave. N., 3rd Floor, (205) 264-1331

Boston, MA 02116, 10th Floor, 441 Stuart St., (617) 223-2312

Buffalo, NY 14202, 1312 Federal Bldg., 111 W. Huron St., (716) 846-4191

Charleston, WV 25301, 3000 New Federal Office Bldg., 500 Quarrier St., (304) 347-5123

Chicago, IL 60603, Room 1406, Mid-Continental Plaza Bldg., 55 E. Monroe St., (312) 353-4450

Cincinnati, OH 45202, 10504 Federal Bldg., 550 Main St., (513) 684-2944

Cleveland, OH 44114, Room 600, 666 Euclid Ave., (216) 522-4750

Columbia, SC 29201, Federal Bldg., 1835 Assembly St., (803) 765-5345

Dallas, TX 75242, Room 7A5, 1100 Commerce St., (214) 767-0542

Denver, CO 80202, Room 177, U.S. Custom House, 721 19th St., (303) 844-3246

Des Moines, IA 50309, 817 Federal Bldg., 210 Walnut St., (515) 284-4222

Detroit, MI 48226, 445 Federal Bldg., 231 W. Lafayette., (313) 226-3650

Greensboro, NC 27402, 203 Federal Bldg., W. Market St., P.O. Box 1950, (919) 378-5345

Hartford, CT 06103, Room 610-B, Federal Bldg., 450 Main St., (203) 244-3530

Honolulu, HI 96850, 4106 Federal Bldg., 300 Ala Moana Blvd., P.O. Box 50026, (808) 546-8694

Houston, TX 77002, 2625 Federal Bldg., 515 Rusk St., (713) 229-2578

Indianapolis, IN 46204, 357 U.S. Courthouse & Federal Bldg., 46 E. Ohio St., (317) 269-6214

Jackson, MS 39213, Suite 328, 300 Woodrow Wilson Rd., (601) 965-4388

Kansas City, MO 64106, Room 1840, Savers Federal Bldg., 601 E. 12th St., (816) 374-3142

Little Rock, AR 72201, Room 635, 320 W. Capitol Ave., (501) 378-5794

Los Angeles, CA 90049, Room 800, 11777 San Vicente Blvd., (213) 209-6707

Louisville, KY 40202, Room 636B, U.S. Post Office and Courthouse Bldg., (502) 582-5066

Miami, FL 33130, 51 S.W. First Ave., (305) 536-5267

Milwaukee, WI 53202, 605 Federal Office Bldg., 517 E. Wisconsin Ave., (414) 291-3473

Minneapolis, MN 55401, 218 Federal Bldg., 110 S. 4th St., (612) 349-3338

Nashville, TN 37239, One Commerce Place, Suite 1427, (615) 251-5161

New Orleans, LA 70130, Room 432, International Trade Mart, 2 Canal St., (504) 589-6546

New York, NY 10278, 37th Floor, Federal Office Bldg., 26 Federal Plaza, Foley Sq., (212) 264-0634

Oklahoma City, OK 73105, 4024 Lincoln Blvd., (405) 231-5302

Omaha, NB 68102, Empire State Bldg., 1st Floor, 300 S. 19th St., (402) 221-3664

Philadelphia, PA 19106, 9448 Federal Bldg., 600 Arch St., (215) 597-2866

Phoenix, AZ 85025, 230 N. 1st Ave., (602) 254-3285

Pittsburgh, PA 15222, 2002 Federal Bldg., 1000 Liberty Ave., (412) 644-2850

Portland, OR 97204, Room 618, 1220 S.W. 3rd Ave., (503) 221-3001

Reno, NV 89502, 1755 E. Plumb La., (702) 784-5203

Richmond, VA 23240, 8010 Federal Bldg., 400 N. 8th St., (804) 771-2246

St. Louis, MO 63105, 120 S. Central Ave., (314) 425-3302

Salt Lake City, UT 84101, Room 340, U.S. Post Office and Courthouse Bldg., 350 S. Main St., (801) 524-5116

San Francisco, CA 94102, Federal Bldg., Box 36013, 450 Golden Gate Ave., (415) 556-5860

San Juan, PR 00918, Room 659, Federal Bldg., Chardon Ave., (809) 753-4555, ext. 555

Savannah, GA 31401, 27 E. Bay St., (912) 944-4204

Seattle, WA 98109, 706 Lake Union Bldg., 1700 Westlake Ave. N., (206) 442-5616

Trenton, NJ 08608, 240 W. State St., (609) 989-2100

If you have a consumer product, register with In-Store Promotion Program, U.S. Department of Commerce, Office of International Marketing, Washington, DC 20230.

Official export statistics of the United States are published by the Bureau of the Census. The report is entitled *FT 410: U.S. Exports of Domestic and Foreign Merchandise, Commodity by Country of Destination*, and is available through ITA/DOC district offices.

Table A-1 summarizes the services and information available from the U.S. Department of Commerce. Use the following key in reading the table:

Potential markets	A
Market research	B
Direct sales leads	C
Agents/distributors	D
Export counseling	E
Export/import regulations	F
Overseas contract opportunities	G
Marketing plans	H

Table A-1. Summary of Services and Information Available from the U.S. Department of Commerce

	A	B	C	D	E	F	G	H
Foreign Trade Statistics	x	x						
Global Market Surveys	x	x						
Market Share Reports	x	x						
Foreign Economic Trends	x	x						
Commercial Exhibitions	x	x	x	x				
Overseas Business Reports	x	x						
Overseas Private Investment Corp		x						
New Product Information Service			x	x				
Trade Opportunities Program			x	x			x	
Export Contact List Services			x	x				
Agent Distributor Service				x				
U.S. Commercial Service	x	x			x	x		
ITA Business Counseling	x	x			x	x		
Export Seminars					x			
U.S. Foreign Commercial Service	x	x	x	x		x	x	x
International Economic Indicators	x	x						
Country Market Sectoral Surveys	x	x						
Office of Country Marketing	x	x	x	x	x	x	x	
East-West Trade	x	x				x		x
Office of Export Administration					x	x		
Small Business Administration					x			
Major Projects Overseas							x	
Worldwide Information and Trade System	x	x	x	x			x	
Product Marketing Service	x	x	x	x				

Organizations of Interest to U.S. Firms

Chamber of Commerce of the United States, 1615 H St., N.W., Washington, DC 20062, (202) 659-6000

Department of State, Bureau of Economic and Business Affairs, 2201 C St., N.W., Washington, DC 20520, (202) 647-7991

The National Council for U.S.-China Trade, 1818 N St., N.W., Washington, DC 20036, (202) 429-0340

U.S. International Trade Commission, 701 E St., N.W., Washington, DC 20004, (202) 523-0161

State Economic Development Offices with Responsibility for International Trade

Alabama Development Office, 3734 Atlanta Highway, Montgomery, AL 36109, (205) 832-6980

Department of Commerce & Economic Development, Pouch D, Juneau, AK 99811, (907) 465-3580

Director of International Trade, Office of Economic Planning & Development, 1700 W. Washington St., Room 505, Phoenix, AZ 85007, (602) 255-3737

Department of Economic Development, 1 Capitol Mall, Room 4C-300, Little Rock, AR 72201, (501) 371-2052

Department of Commerce & Development, 1313 Sherman St., Room 500, Denver, CO 80203, (303) 839-2552

International Division, Department of Economic Development, 210 Washington St., Hartford, CT 06106, (203) 566-3842

Economic Development, Box 1401, 99 King's Highway, Dover, DE 19903, (302) 736-4254

Bureau of Trade Development, Division of Economic Development, Department of Commerce, Collins Building, Tallahassee, FL 32301, (904) 488-6124

International Trade Division, Department of Industry & Trade, P.O. Box 1776, Atlanta, GA 30301, (404) 656-3746

International Services Agency, Dept. of Planning & Economic Development, Financial Plaza of the Pacific, 130 Merchant St., Honolulu, HA 96813, (808) 548-3048 (or 548-4621)

Division of Economic & Community Affairs, State Capitol, Boise, ID 83720, (208) 334-2470

Marketing Bureau, Dept. of Commerce & Community Affairs, 100 W. Randolph, Chicago IL 62706, (217) 782-6861

International Trade Division, Department of Commerce, 1 N. Capitol, Indianapolis, IN 46204, (317) 232-8845 (or 8846)

International Division, Iowa Development Commission, 600 E. Court Ave., Des Moines, IA 50309, (515) 281-3251

International Trade Development Division, Kansas Dept. of Economic Development, 400 W. 8th St., Topeka, KS 66603, (913) 296-3483

International Trade Division, Kentucky Department of Commerce, Capital Plaza Tower, Frankfort, KY 40601, (502) 564-2170

International Division, Office of Commerce & Industry, 343 International Trade Mart, New Orleans, LA 70130, (504) 568-5255

State Development Office, State House, Station #59, Augusta, ME 04333, (207) 289-2656

Office of Business & Industrial Development, Department of Economic & Community Development, 1748 Forest Dr., Annapolis, MD 21401, (301) 269-3514

International Operations Division, Michigan Department of Commerce, Law Building, 5th Floor, Lansing, MI 48909, (517) 373-6390

Department of Economic Development, 150 E. Kellogg Blvd., St. Paul, MN 55101, (612) 296-2755

International Business Development, P.O. Box 849, Jackson, MS 39205, (601) 354-6707

International Business Office, Division of Community & Economic Development, P.O. Box 118, Jefferson City, MO 65102, (314) 751-4855

Governor's Office of Commerce & Small Business Development, State Capitol, Helena, MT 59620, (406) 449-3923

Industrial Development Division, Department of Economic Development, P.O. Box 94666, Lincoln, NE 68509, (402) 471-3111

Department of Economic Development, Capitol Complex, Carson City, NV 89710, (702) 885-4322

Foreign Trade & Commercial Development, Dept. of Resources & Economic Development, P.O. Box 856, Concord, NH 03301, (603) 271-2591

Department of Labor & Industry, John Fitch Plaza, Trenton, NJ 08625, (609) 292-2323

International Trade Development, Department of Commerce & Industry, 1100 St. Francis Dr., Santa Fe, NM 87503, (505) 827-5571

Division of International Commerce, 230 Park Ave., NY 10169, (212) 309-0513. International Division, Department of Commerce, 430 N. Salisbury St., Raleigh, NC 27611, (919) 733-7193

Division of International Trade, Department of Commerce, 30 E. Broad St., 25th Floor, Columbus, OH 43215, (614) 466-5017

International Trade Division, Department of Industrial Development, 4024 N. Lincoln Blvd., Oklahoma City, OK 73105, (405) 521-3501

Department of Economic Development, 1500 S.W. First, Portland, OR 97201, (503) 229-5625 or (800) 452-7813

Bureau of International Development, Department of Commerce, 450 Forum Bldg., Harrisburg, PA 17120, (717) 787-7190

Department of Economic Development, 7 Jackson Walkway, Providence, RI 02903, (401) 277-2605

Business & Economic Development, Box 927, Columbia, SC 29202, (803) 758-2235

Industrial Development Expansion Agency, 221 South Central, Pierre, SD 57501, (605) 773-5037

Office of Export Promotion, Andrew Jackson Bldg., #1021, Nashville, TN 37219, (615) 741-5870

Texas Industrial Commission, P.O. Box 12728, Capitol Station, Austin, TX 78711, (512) 472-5059

International Business & Industrial Training, Economic Development Department, Agency of Development & Community Affairs, Pavilion Office Bldg., 109 State St., Montpelier, VT 05602, (802) 828-3221

International Trade & Development, Division of Industrial Development, 1010 State Office Bldg., Richmond, VA 23219, (804) 786-3791

Trade Development, Department of Commerce & Economic Development, 312 First Ave. N., Seattle, WA 98109, (206) 464-7076

Trade Administration, Department of Commerce, Charleston, WV 25304, (304) 343-6181

Department of Business Development, 123 W. Washington Ave., Madison, WI 53702, (608) 266-3222

Industrial Division, Department of Economic Planning & Development, Herschler Bldg., Cheyenne, WY 82002, (307) 777-7285

International Commodity Codes

Trade statistics in most countries utilize commodity codes rather than spell out products by category or title. The most widely used are the SITC (Standard International Trade Classification) and the BTN (Brussels Trade Nomenclature) codes. You can get a directory of SITC codes with correlated BTN equivalents from the United Nations, Sales Section, U.N. Plaza, New York, NY 10017. Order *Standard International Trade Classification Revision 2*, Sales No. E.75.XVII.6, ST/ESA/STAT/SER.M/34/Rev2.

Military PX/Commissary Organizations

If you have a product to offer the PX/Commissary market, get a copy of *Vendor Facts*, Army and Air Force Exchange Service, Red Bird Plaza, Dallas, TX 75222; subscribe to *Exchange and Commissary News*, P.O. Box 788, Lynbrook NY 11563, and *Military Market*, 475 School St., Washington, DC 20024.

The largest military reps belong to the Armed Forces Marketing Council (955 L'Enfant Plaza N., Washington, DC 20006). Write for a list; specify your type of product.

Headquarters for the PX System

Army & Air Force Exchange Service, Red Bird Plaza, Dallas, TX 75222, (214) 330-3721

Marine Corps Exchange Service Division, Headquarters, U.S. Marine Corps, Bldg. No. 3074, MCB Quantico, VA 22134, (703) 640-2917

Navy Resale System Office, Code CO 6, Fort Wadsworth, NY 10305

Navy Resale System Office, West Coast, Bldg. 310, Naval Supply Center, Oakland, CA 94625, (415) 466-5733

Headquarters for the Commissary System

Air Force Commissary Stores, Director of Supply & Services, Kelly Air Force Base, Kelly, TX 78241, (512) 925-7958

Army Commissary Stores, Commissary Branch, Troop Support Division, Department of the Army (DALO-SMT-C), Room 1E-573A, The Pentagon, Washington, DC 20310. (202) OX5-9001 or OX7-4322

Coast Guard Commissary Stores, Resale Programs Branch Headquarters, U.S. Coast Guard, Room 5310, 2100 Second St., Washington, DC 20590, (202) 426-2094

Marine Corps Commissary Stores, 1300 Wilson Blvd., Rosslyn, VA 22209, (703) 694-8616

Foreign Embassies

You should subscribe to the *Diplomatic List*. This quarterly publication contains the addresses of all foreign embassies in Washington, as well as the names of the members of diplomatic staffs. Annual subscription: $3. Order from Superintendent of Documents, U.S. Government Printing Office, Washington, DC 20402. Refer to Department of State Publication No. 7894.

Associations of Export Management Companies in the United States

Contact these associations for names and addresses of U.S. exporters and export management companies. Ask also for names and addresses of similar associations in major industrialized countries, particularly in Western Europe, since some of their members could be good outlets into specific markets.

Export Managers Association of California, 14549 Victory Blvd., Van Nuys CA 91411, (213) 479-3911

Overseas Sales and Marketing Association of America, Inc., P.O. Box 45446, Chicago, IL 60645, (312) 583-6060

National Association of Export Management Companies Inc, 65 Liberty St., New York, NY 10005, (212) 766-1343

Pacific Northwest Association of Export Managers, 5316 S.W. Westgate Dr., Portland, OR 97211, (503) 292-9219

Foreign Chambers of Commerce in the United States

Contact the following for advice on possible overseas agents and to get names and addresses of counterpart chambers of commerce in their countries.

The Finnish-American Chamber of Commerce, 15th Floor, 540 Madison Ave., New York, NY 10022, (212) 832-2588

French-American Chamber of Commerce in the U.S., 509 Madison Ave., New York, NY 10022, (212) 581-4554

The Finnish-American Chamber of Commerce of the Midwest, Suite 1900, 35 E. Wacker Dr., Chicago, IL 60601, (312) 346-1150

German-American Chamber of Commerce, Inc., 666 Fifth Ave., New York, NY 10103, (212) 582-7788

German-American Chamber of Commerce of Chicago, 104 S. Michigan Ave., Chicago, IL 60603, (312) 782-8557

German-American Chamber of Commerce of Los Angeles, Inc., Suite 2212, One Park Plaza Bldg., 3250 Wilshire Blvd., Los Angeles, CA 90010, (213) 381-2236

German-American Chamber of Commerce of the Pacific Coast, Inc., Suite 910, 465 California St., San Francisco, CA 94104, (415) 392-2262

German-American Chamber of Commerce, Suite 606, One Farragut Square S., Washington, DC 20006, (202) 347-0247

Italy-America Chamber of Commerce, Inc., Suite 3015, 350 Fifth Ave., New York, NY 10118, (212) 279-5520

The Netherlands Chamber of Commerce in the U.S., Inc., 11th Floor, One Rockefeller Plaza, New York, NY 10020, (212) 265-6460

Spain-U.S. Chamber of Commerce, 350 Fifth Ave., New York, NY 10118, (212) 967-2170

Spain-U.S. Chamber of Commerce of the Pacific Coast, Suite 944, World Trade Center, 350 S. Figueroa St., Los Angeles, CA 90071, (213) 489-4459

Swedish-American Chamber of Commerce of the Western U.S., Inc., Suite 268, Ferry Bldg., World Trade Center, San Francisco, CA 94101, (415) 781-4188

British-American Chamber of Commerce, 275 Madison Ave., New York, NY 94111, (212) 889-0680

United Nations and Other International Organizations

Write each organization, ask to be placed on their mailing list for any project announcements pertaining to your product category, send catalogs and prices for reference. Use as sources of intelligence.

UN/United Nations, Chief Purchase and Transportation Service, New York, NY 10017

ILO/International Labor Organization, Chief Bureau for the Coordination of Operational Activities, International Labour Office, Geneva 22, Switzerland

FAO/Food and Agriculture Organization, Chief Purchasing and Control Branch, Administrative Services Division, Food and Agriculture Organization of the United Nations, via delle terme di Caracalla, Rome, Italy

UNESCO/United Nations Educational, Scientific and Cultural Organization, Director UNESCO Field Equipment Division, UNESCO, 7 Place de Fontenoy, 75700 Paris, France

ICAO/International Civil Aviation Organization, Director Technical Assistance Bureau, Montreal 101, Canada

WHO/World Health Organization, Deputy Director General, World Health Organization, Avenue Appia, Geneva 22, Switzerland

ITU/International Telecommunications Union, The Secretary General, International Telecommunications Union, 1211 Geneva 20, Switzerland

IAEA/International Atomic Energy Agency, Division of Technical Assistance, International Atomic Energy Agency, Kaerntnerring 11, A-1010 Vienna 1, Austria

UNIDO/United Nations Industrial Development Organization, Chief Purchasing and Contracting Services, UNIDO, P.O. Box 707, A-1011 Vienna, Austria

WMO/World Meteorological Organization, Director Technical Co-operation Department, World Meteorological Organization, P.O. Box No. 5, CH-1211 Geneva 20, Switzerland

UNDP/United Nations Development Programme, Director Office for Projects Execution, United Nations Development Programme, New York, New York 10017

ADB/Asian Development Bank, P.O. Box 789, Metro Manila, Philippines

ADFAED/Abu Dhabi Fund for Arab Economic Development, P.O. Box 814, Abu Dhabi, United Arab Emirates

AfDB/African Development Bank, B.P. 1387, Abidjan 01, Ivory Coast

Arab Fund for Economic and Social Development, P.O. Box 21923, Kuwait

BADEA/Banque Arabe de Developpement Economique en Afrique, P.O. Box 2640, Baladia Road, Khartoum, Sudan

BOAD/Banque Ouest Africaine de Developpement, P.O. Box 1172, Lome, Togo

CABEI/Central American Bank for Economic Integration, Apartado Postal 772, Tegucigalpa, Honduras

CDB/Caribbean Development Bank, P.O. Box 408, Wildey, St Michael, Barbados

IFC/International Finance Corporation, 1818 H St., N.W., Washington, DC 20433

IMF/International Monetary Fund, 700 19th St., N.W., Washington, DC 20431

Islamic Development Bank, Al-Niaba Palace, Jeddah, Saudi Arabia

KFAED/Kuwait Fund for Arab Economic Development, P.O. Box 2921, Kuwait

OAS/Organization of American States, General Secretariat, 1889 F St., N.W., Washington, DC 20006

OPEC/Organization of Petroleum Exporting Countries, Special Fund, P.O. Box 995, A-1011 Vienna, Austria

Saudi Fund for Development, P.O. Box 50483, Riyadh, Saudi Arabia

UNICEF/United Nations Children's Fund, 866 UN Plaza, New York, NY 10017

USAID/United States Agency for International Development, 320 21st St., N.W., Washington, DC 20520

World Bank (IBRD), 1818 H St., N.W., Washington, DC 20433

Index

About the Author

Erik Wiklund has more than 25 years' experience in international marketing in a variety of capacities from export salesman to consultant. His impressive roster of clients includes companies from the United States, European nations, Japan, and Australia. The author of *International Marketing: Making Exports Pay Off* (McGraw-Hill), Mr. Wiklund also publishes a newsletter about foreign markets.